IRELAND'S SH

Ireland's Shannon Story

*Leaders, Visions and Networks –
A Case Study of Local and
Regional Development*

BRIAN CALLANAN

IRISH ACADEMIC PRESS
DUBLIN • PORTLAND, OR

First published in 2000 by
IRISH ACADEMIC PRESS
44, Northumberland Road, Dublin 4, Ireland
and in the United States of America by
IRISH ACADEMIC PRESS
c/o ISBS, 5804 NE Hassalo Street, Portland, OR 97213.

website: www.iap.ie

British Library Cataloguing in Publication Data
Callanan, Brian
  Ireland's Shannon story : leaders, visions and networks – a case study of local and
  regional development
  1. Shannon Development   2. Regional planning – Ireland – Shannon
  I. Title
  307.1'4'09417
  ISBN 0–7165–2710–3 hbk
       0–7165–2643–3 pbk

Library of Congress Cataloging-in-Publication Data
Callanan, Brian, 1949–
  Ireland's Shannon Story: leaders, visions, and networks : a case study of local and
  regional development / Brian Callanan.
      p.   cm.
  Includes bibliographical references and index.
  ISBN 0–7165–2710–3 (hbk.). — ISBN 0–7165–2643–3 (pbk.)
    1. City planning—Ireland—Shannon—History.   2. Regional planning—
  Ireland—Shannon—History.   I. Title.
  HT 169.I78S533   2000
  307.76'094193—DC21   99–10073
                                                                  CIP

Typeset in 11.25 pt on 13 pt Bembo by
Carrigboy Typesetting Services, County Cork
Printed by
Creative Print and Design, (Wales), Ebbw Vale

Contents

List of Maps and Illustrations

All Maps and Illustrations (between pages 110–111) are courtesy of Shannon Development.

MAPS

ILLUSTRATIONS

List of Figures

Foreword

THE SHANNON Development agency (SFADCo) has attracted widespread interest throughout the world from those concerned with innovative public management and economic development. Brian Callanan has produced the first major case study that combines the knowledge of an insider with the analytical skills of a qualified social scientist. With the advantage of access to archive material, he has been able to tell the 'Shannon story' with unprecedented directness and attention to historical detail. He also has the ability to place that detail in a larger theoretical significance for political and social change beyond the Irish context.

The substance of the book was presented successfully as a thesis for Doctor of Philosophy at the University of Limerick. The thesis was very much influenced by the idea of 'associative capacity', which I proposed in the context of the European Commission's action research in local employment development. Brian cleverly elaborated upon this idea, and produced evidence for it, presenting Shannon Development as exemplary of an 'alternative paradigm' or third way of solving problems in post-industrial economies. He has thus made a contribution of much greater moment for both theory and practice than his modesty allows him to claim. I am privileged to introduce this book, which makes a solid and lasting recognition of the extraordinary individual and collective endeavours that produced such a remarkable Irish contribution to development in both a European and a global context.

DAVID COOMBES
Professor of European Studies
University of Limerick
June, 1999

Introduction

JAMES GRANT seemed vexed. Writing in a review of developments in Scotland's Highlands he wrote with apparent exasperation:

> The intervention of governments to help under-developed or distressed areas is generally based on ideology, or political pressure, or on someone's hunch. We need a much more scientific approach to these matters, based on practical experience in the field.[1]

This study attempts to take up the challenge posed by Grant. The study, using the practical experience of Shannon Free Airport Development Company (SFADCo) in Ireland during the 1957–85 period, tries to draw some systematic conclusions from the work of the agency. The research technique is that of the 'case study' method. The study is in three parts: the first outlines the field of regional development both in theory and practice; the second provides the practical case study of the SFADCo experience; the third part reflects on what the experience adds to the field of knowledge of regional development.

The first part opens with a review of the experience of four agencies in regional development – the Tennessee Valley Authority (USA), the Cassa per Il Mezzogiorno (Italy), the Highlands and Islands Development Board (Scotland) and the Congested Districts Board (Ireland). Following that review, the field of regional development is examined with its diverse themes and debates, particularly the two paradigms (or theories) of development from above and development from below. We also examine growth poles, cumulative causation, transitional regions and self-reliant development. To this is added an outline of organisational aspects, indicating issues from administrative life that need to be addressed. These include matters arising within organisations (such as learning, entrepreneurship, leadership) and within the wider social environment (such as laws, power, interdependence, networking).

From these three standpoints of agencies, development theory and organisation, the research issues are briefly summarised. These issues are the role of leaders and personalities in regional development, how goals and visions are defined and the relationships of the agencies with other groups at local and national level.

The second part – the case study – presents the SFADCo experience: the background to the establishment of the agency, tourism projects, industrial free zone, new town, regional industry, small industry, alternative evaluations. While this is a descriptive account, a number of general themes and issues assert themselves, for example how policy differences are reconciled by local alliances and coalitions, managing institutional conflicts, local empowerment, industrial clusters, informal networks, integrating grand visions with a step by step approach.

The third and final part attempts to draw systematic conclusions from the case study. Critically, the two paradigms of development from above and development from below are found to be inadequate with neither fully explaining the story. Consequently, a need arises for a third paradigm that embraces more fully the irregularities and discontinuities inherent in regional development. The third paradigm could evolve through building blocks arising from practical experiences, with three such elements singled out by the present case study as deserving particular attention:

• Personal leadership within a supportive environment of policy and administration.
• Visions that define a desired future state of affairs in an exciting manner.
• Networks of personal contacts that are diffused over diverse groups and categories of people.

The research method used in this study has been that of the 'case study'.[2] Case study research follows a series of steps:

• Study design
• Preparing for data collection
• Collecting the evidence
• Analysing the evidence
• Composing the report

To be successful, case studies need to display several characteristics. Four in particular have been singled out. We will look at these now.

Significant

The case study must be significant. It should be of some unusual item of public interest, with underlying issues of national or international importance.

It could be a revelatory case, revealing some potential discovery or example of something. Alternatively, the case study could be used to test alternative theoretical propositions about a phenomenon, assessing the relevance of different theories in the light of their applicability to a specific piece of reality.

Complete

The case study must be complete. There are three dimensions to this. Firstly, there must be a clear boundary around the case under investigation. This boundary could be in terms of a time period, or spatial area, or group of people. The boundary should be logical and relevant with meaning and sense.

Secondly, the case study should expend exhaustive effort in collecting relevant evidence. No available material should be left untouched thus convincing the reader that all the material has been addressed. Of course, this does not mean the collection or use of all the available evidence: this would be impossible. But the critical pieces have to be given complete attention, especially the exploration of any elements that represent rival propositions, conclusions or explanations.

Thirdly, there should be no artificial, or non-research, constraints. If the researchers have to curtail the study because of time pressures or resource constraints, then the case study will be less than exemplary. Of course, there are always resource and other external constraints that restrict researchers. But the way to handle those limitations is to design the case study within them from the start. Thus the case study is designed as 'complete' within the resource framework at the very beginning.

Alternative propositions

The case study must consider alternative opinions, examining rival propositions and analysing the evidence in the light of these different viewpoints. There is always a danger that the investigators will only collect evidence that supports a single point of view, ignoring material that justifies an alternative explanation. Even if the researchers are not biased, contrasting interpretations must be consciously entertained, with a positive search for alternatives that challenge the assumptions behind the case study design. If this is done systematically, then the range of evidence considered will be substantially more complete, presenting the different points of view of all the major actors.

Sufficient evidence

The case study must contain sufficient evidence. The critical pieces of evidence must be contained within the report. The exemplary case study is one that judiciously and effectively presents the most compelling evidence, enabling a reader to make an independent judgement regarding the merits of the analysis. The evidence should be presented neutrally, with both supporting and challenging data so that the reader can conclude – independently – whether a particular interpretation is valid. This selectiveness in the evidence does not mean that researchers are biased, but that the material is limited to the most critical evidence and is not cluttered with secondary information.

The material should also be sufficient to allow a 'chain of evidence' to be built up, allowing the reader to follow the logic from study design, to data, to analysis, to conclusions. The external reader should be able to trace the steps in either direction – from design to conclusion, and back again. Such a chain of evidence will quickly demonstrate the existence of any bias in a case study.

Setting out these qualities of an exemplary case study illustrates what the study is trying to achieve. It shows what best practice is and provides a yardstick by which the present study can be evaluated. It also highlights the difficulties and pitfalls involved in doing good case studies. It does not at all suggest that this research secures these goals or meets these criteria, but it does provide a useful framework for judging and appraising the study.

The case study was undertaken over four years, 1990–94. The case was the history of SFADCo during 1957–85, the time in which the organisation's programmes were developed and managed by the 'founding fathers' of the agency. The 'phenomenon' it represents is the process of local and regional development, and in particular the institutional aspects of that process.

The case study was undertaken in a number of phases.

1. The initial research proposal was prepared in consultation with the University of Limerick. Discussions were also held at this stage with the key actors from SFADCo who provided helpful insights into the appropriate goals and methodology of the study.
2. This preparation was followed by archival investigation of internal documentation, correspondence, reports and minutes of meetings. A preliminary working paper was prepared following the archival search and shown to both University personnel and key actors. Comments and criticisms were received.

3. This was followed by a second phase of investigation involving searching interviews with key actors. The issues highlighted in the documentary stage provide a central framework for the face-to-face discussions.

4. Following the interview phase, a draft report was prepared with preliminary conclusions. This was also shown to key actors who commented critically.

5. Subsequently, a final version of the research report was completed.

This process was useful on two counts. Firstly, dividing the data collection into two distinct phases of documentation and interviews allowed for the fullest use of both sources in a complementary manner. Secondly, involving the key actors in commenting on the drafts enabled a number of perspectives and interpretations to enter the picture. Thus the people who participated in the subject of the case study actively assisted in the research conclusions. Of course, the opinions expressed in this final report, and any errors or omissions, remain the author's responsibility.

The study would not have been possible without the advice and help of many people. The original idea for the research came from Professor Patrick O'Farrell of Heriot-Watt University (Edinburgh). Professor O'Farrell's suggestion was for an investigation by archival search and interviews of the SFADCo experiences within the framework of regional development. Professor David Coombes of the University of Limerick elaborated this further, with particular reference to 'capacity for association' as an ingredient in regional change.

The people involved in SFADCo at the time provided wonderful advice and support through access to archives and information and by giving valuable time for interview. These people were Brendan O'Regan, Paul Quigley, the late Peter Donnelly, Tom Callanan and Jack Lynch. Without their understanding and insights this study would have been impossible.

Other useful interviews were given by Des O'Malley TD, and Fr Harry Bohan. Staff at the University of Limerick provided helpful information and advice, namely Professor Noel Mulcahy, John Stapleton, Professor Nick Rees, Pattie Punch and Martina Flynn. Other advice was also given by Professor Jim Walsh (NUI, Maynooth), Professor Frances Ruane (TCD) and Professor Peter Neary (UCD).

Drafts of the study were typed by Deirdre Phelan and Mary Lawlor. Everlasting love and support was given by Sheila, Jill, Hilary and Ronan.

BRIAN CALLANAN
Shannon Development
June, 1999

I

Agencies in Regional Development

ONE

The Agencies

THE NATURE and definition of regional development agencies has varied over time and from place to place.

We can define them as organisations concerned with economic development at the local or regional level, and providing a middle ground between public authorities in charge of the collective interest (e.g. elected regional or local councils) and the private sector whose initiative rests on individual interest.[1]

Regional development agencies thus occupy a vague position somewhere between the official organs of regional and local government, and the informal private sector. This position can be described as follows. Agencies of government can be classified according to their representation (elected or not elected), and whether they have competence over a single function (such as water supply, education or housing) or are general purpose agencies. General purpose government has competence over a range of functions that allows a level of political discretion and priorities to be developed between one function and another.[2] This is illustrated in Figure 1 below.

Our interest in regional development agencies is therefore in the bottom right hand quarter: those agencies at a local or regional level which are special purpose and outside the mainstream of local representative government. In some cases, these report directly to central government; in other

FIGURE 1

TYPES OF LOCAL GOVERNMENT

	Representative	*Non-representative*
General purpose	Local representative government	Non-representative local administration
Special purpose	Representative single function districts	**Decentralised agencies**

cases they may be subsidiaries of, or partially owned by, local or regional administration.

This type of administrative structure has a number of benefits. By being on hand to study the problems and having a greater understanding of the economic, social and cultural factors involved, regional and local authorities have a big advantage over central government in some areas of regional policy. However, local and regional governments have all too often fallen into the trap of reproducing at regional level the same kind of bureaucratic problems that have bedevilled central administration for years, so reducing the practical effectiveness of their own regional policy initiatives.

Regional development agencies have been added to the lists of traditional regional policy agents, bringing with them new methods and means of intervention as well as, in some areas, a far greater versatility and capability for action than the public authorities could ever hope to achieve.[3] However, this type of 'third-sector' organisation can be criticised. Writing from the standpoint of the USA, Tierney[4] looks at government corporations in general and argues that relatively little is known about how these organisations are formed, and how and why they behave the way they do. He suggests that there is relatively little to go on in answering even the most obvious questions, warning that if government corporations are to be an increasing feature of public organisation, more should be known about what to expect of them. Tierney voices concerns about deviations from policy, political disquiet and dashed public expectations that could be associated with non-representative government corporations.

Regional development agencies are an established part of the administrative landscape in Europe. The European Association of Development Agencies (EURADA) was established in 1990 to provide a focal point for development agencies in Europe and by 1993 it had almost 100 members.

FIGURE 2

EUROPEAN ASSOCIATION OF DEVELOPMENT AGENCIES:
1993 MEMBERSHIP[5]

Austria	1	Italy	3
Belgium	8	Netherlands	4
Denmark	4	Portugal	3
France	34	Spain	8
Germany	5	Switzerland	1
Greece	6	United Kingdom	20
Ireland	2		

Variations in the volume of members is considerable, with Britain and France being relatively dominant. Germany and Italy have few members, reflecting differences in government and administration in the various countries. In Germany, for example, most development work is carried out directly by organs of provincial or local government. In contrast, in Britain and France much of this work has been delegated to enterprise boards or 'comités d'expansion' respectively, although frequently linked to local government structures.

Four organisations have been picked to provide an overview of issues affecting regional development agencies:

- Tennessee Valley Authority (USA)
- Cassa per il Mezzogiorno (Italy)
- Highland and Islands Development Board (Scotland)
- Congested Districts Board (Ireland)

They have been chosen for three reasons. Firstly, they are relatively old, having been established in the 1930s (Tennessee), the 1950s (Cassa) and the 1960s (Highlands). The Congested Districts Board existed in the late nineteenth and early twentieth centuries. All four thus display a considerable time period over which lessons may be drawn. Secondly, the regional problems they attempted to tackle were relatively large-scale and attracted national attention. They all incorporated a significant range of experience. Thirdly, because of both the previous issues, there exists a substantial body of literature in the form of reports, studies and critical appraisals from which material may be drawn.

The four organisations are thus case studies out of which ideas may be gleaned. They are not necessarily representative of the general body of development agencies. For example, all four were organs of central government, reflecting their national significance and importance. In contrast, most other development agencies are subsidiaries of regional and local government and thus reflect a different political and administrative context.

The Tennessee Valley Authority

The Tennessee Valley Authority, or TVA as it came to be called, has been cited by many as the original prototype of the regional development agency model.[6]

TVA was established in 1933 as part of the 'New Deal' policies of Franklin Delanor Roosevelt to tackle the Great Depression. The TVA Act of that year gave the Authority power to:

- Improve the navigability and flood control of the Tennessee River.
- Provide for reforestation and proper use of marginal levels in the Tennessee Valley.
- Provide for agricultural and industrial development in the area.

TVA thus represented a unique coming together of several strands of development, all linked to the Tennessee River – improving navigation, flood control, hydroelectricity conversion, fertiliser production, agriculture and industry.

Presenting the TVA Bill to Congress in 1933, Roosevelt summed up his vision as:

> potential public usefulness of the entire Tennessee River. Such use, if envisioned in its entirety, transcends mere power development; it enters the wide fields of flood control, soil erosion, afforestation, elimination from agricultural use of marginal lands, and distribution and diversification of industry . . . planning for a complete river watershed involving many states and the future lives and welfare of millions . . . a return to the spirit of the pioneer.[7]

TVA was structured as an authority reporting directly to the US President. The area covered by TVA embraced 40,000 square miles of the Tennessee Valley over several states including Tennessee, Alabama and Kentucky with a population numbering three million. The area was mainly rural with low incomes, marginal agriculture and difficult and inhospitable terrain.

Over the following fifty years, TVA embarked on a series of substantial development measures:

- Navigation: An eleven foot channel was dredged through the 650 miles of the Tennessee River, linking it with the Mississippi system, and providing for annual river traffic of 33 million tonnes.
- Flood Control: 37 dams were constructed along the river to control water levels, reducing flood levels by an estimated 98%.
- Power: Hydroelectric stations were constructed on several of the dams, rural electrification was promoted and coal and nuclear power plants were also developed. Today, over 80,000 square miles are serviced with electricity from TVA sources.
- Agriculture: Provision of low cost power to farms, promotion of fertiliser usage, advisory services and demonstration projects.

- Industry: Development of industrial estates in cooperation with local municipalities.

Economic growth in the Valley has been reported to be substantial.[8] Employment grew from 200,000 to 800,000 over the 1933–83 period, and per capita income in the Valley grew from 40% to 80% of the national average.

Throughout its life, TVA developed a set of ideas or organisational doctrines that clarified its assumptions and approach to the task – an approach that influenced subsequent thinking on regional development. The TVA idea has five essential components:

1. Unified regional development: Holistic approach to resource utilisation and coordination of technical activities, democratic planning and cooperation with others.
2. Decentralised administration: Flexibility, sensitivity, independent action, responsiveness to local needs.
3. People participation: Involvement with the 'grass roots', alliances with local interests and consultation with community groups.
4. Social responsibility: Concern about social issues, skills training, educational programmes and community revitalisation.
5. Non-political policy making: Commitment to merit and technical principles in decision making and the separation of politics from administration.[9]

TVA was thus an organisation with considerable vision and ambition. It was also substantial in scale, employing 13,000 people and having annual expenditure of over $4,000 million. Evidently, such a size and scope attracted considerable criticisms, some of which are worth summarising.

TVA appears to have enjoyed much support both nationally and from the people in the valley up to the early 1970s but from then on, the Authority entered realms of controversy. Three particular issues of contention have been highlighted:

- Firstly, TVA was criticised for strip mining and air pollution and faced conflict with the environmental movement.
- Secondly, TVA engaged in a number of large scale water projects that stimulated heavy conflicts with local communities.
- Thirdly, after the first oil crisis of 1974, TVA entered a period of nuclear power station construction, and was criticised for producing an expensive plant in excess of needs.[10]

TVA's so-called 'grass roots' approach also came under fire. Although concerned about local commitment, TVA has been accused of encouraging an excessive dependency on cheap electricity, virtually eliminating alternative energy and engendering excessive expectations among local communities.[11]

Accountability at TVA has been a significant area of debate, generating the question of who is TVA accountable to. Technically, it reported directly to the President but the powers of Congress, the State legislation and the Valley people were inadequately defined. But it is also recognised that accountability needs to be balanced against the need for flexibility and independence of the organisation.[12]

Others have argued that the TVA is really a power-generation organisation and that claims for regional development have been exaggerated. For example, power generation comprised 94% of the TVA annual budget, with only 6% for flood control, agriculture and industrial development.[13]

The grass roots doctrine of TVA has been studied sociologically by Philip Selznick,[14] investigating the meaning of this approach, and what effect this theory had on the moral posture and competence of TVA as a government agency. Selznick's conclusion was that the grass roots doctrine resulted in a serious weakening of the TVA's capacity to be a front-line, committed conservation agency. He made five specific observations:

1. The grass roots theory became a protective ideology. TVA acted as a champion of local institutions but this distanced the Authority from federal departments. As a consequence, hostility was engendered and these departments opposed the extension of TVA-type organisations to other areas.

2. The agriculture programme of TVA was heavily determined by local interest groups within the Valley, and this sucked the TVA into a type of 'constituency' relationship with them.

3. This allied TVA with pressure groups in conflict with national agricultural authorities, and further distanced TVA from potential allies at national level.

4. Under pressure from local agricultural groups, TVA was weakened as a conservation agency. The policy of public ownership of land was resisted by these agricultural groups, and this affected TVA's approach to the issue.

5. The grass roots doctrine of involving voluntary associations was not really a sharing of power at all. Rather it was a means of generating support for the TVA development programme, with power and authority remaining in the hands of TVA.

To conclude on TVA, we can agree that it was substantial not only in its visions and its achievements, but also in the criticism it attracted. Perhaps these are linked. TVA was a large organisation, locally based with a multi-sectoral approach and driven by a set of imaginative goals; it was also a new experimental type of venture outside the conventional mainstream of federal and state government. Such an arrangement would inevitably attract significant debate and criticism.

Cassa per il Mezzogiorno

The development problem in Italy has been dominated by gross economic distortions between the North and the South. The South is called the 'Mezzogiorno', or 'Land of the Noon-Day Sun'.

The Mezzogiorno region with a population of eighteen million embraces the entire southern half of the Italian peninsula below Naples, together with Sicily and Sardinia. In the 1940s it displayed a series of problems that had beset the area for some generations – very low per capita income relative to the North (60%), high emigration, poor infrastructure and weak industry. Farming was typified by feudal-style land ownership, a source of considerable social tension.

Initial measures to cope with these problems were concentrated on land reform. During the 1940s, as many as 700,000 hectares were redistributed to farm labourers and peasants. The motivation for most of these measures was political with the ruling Christian Democrat Party fearing the inroads of the Communists. Land reform, and the creation of a proprietorial class of small farmers, was a means of resisting such encroachment.[15]

A new policy departure was announced in 1950 with the creation of the Bank for Extraordinary Works in the Public Interest in Southern Italy (Cassa per il Mezzogiorno) providing a coordinated approach instead of earlier fragmented action. These earlier measures were seen to lack clear aims and directions. The preamble to the Cassa legislation stated that there was a need for a new body to implement the development programme with consistent policies, technical planning expertise and close attention to economic and social issues.[16] The Cassa was to be concerned with 'extraordinary interventions' i.e. special development measures outside the mainstream of conventional public expenditure.

Distinctive features of the Cassa were that it was to be free of cumbersome procedures, have access to technical skills, be intersectoral in nature, embrace the different specialisms of several ministers and enjoy the flexibility of a budget planned over several years. The Cassa reported to an interministerial committee for the Mezzogiorno.[17]

The first phase of the Cassa's life (1951–57) concentrated almost exclusively on land reform, agricultural development and general infrastructure through reclamation, reallocation of land ownership, drainage and communications. But the expected economic progress did not materialise. Cassa expenditure turned out to be a substitution for ordinary public expenditure, rather than an addition to it; the agricultural programmes did not give the required impetus to growth in incomes. Consequently, in 1957, the activities of the Cassa were expanded to include industrial development, incorporating three major components:

- A growth centre policy was adopted with the designation of specific growth areas and the identification of other nuclei for the location of industry. In these areas, so-called 'Consortia' could be established: organs of local government to plan and develop industrial investment with the financial support of the Cassa.
- Incentives were provided such as tax concessions, capital grants and interest subsidies.
- The state manufacturing sector was directed to locate a prescribed proportion of new investment in the Mezzogiorno.

The purpose of the Cassa growth centre policy was to build up external economies approaching those of more advanced industrial regions. Growth centres would provide enterprises locating in them with proximity to complementary industries, availability of services and diversified labour market. There was some debate about the designation of growth centres and a two-tier policy was adopted: 'areas' for industrialisation (over 200,000 population) and 'nuclei' (with less than 75,000 population). Criteria for selection included previous growth record, prospects for future expansion and availability of services. Preferential treatment was given for areas and nuclei in the granting of incentives.

The 'Consortia' comprised representatives from local government, chambers of commerce and others who drew up a planning scheme for their area within a general framework laid down by the Cassa. The Cassa aimed to be considerably decentralised. Apart from the local Consortia, other bodies were set up under the aegis of the Cassa to develop related programmes, such as agencies to support local entrepreneurs and provide industrial training.

During the 1970s, efforts were intensified to secure a more coordinated approach to the development of the Mezzogiorno. This involved two particular approaches: greater unity of public action within the Mezzogiorno, and stronger national planning to favour the South. For local integration, the Cassa was responsible for the preparation of a series of the five year plans to bring together interventions in industry, agriculture and tourism. At national level, a series of national economic programmes established targets to narrow the gap between the North and South of Italy.

In the sphere of agriculture, the Cassa continued to operate significant programmes such as irrigation, afforestation, land reclamation, rural water supply, electricity distribution, rural housing and the consolidation of small marginal holdings into larger properties. Tourism was assisted through capital grants and loan subsidies for hotels and local tourist development, with a concentration of effort on selected tourist areas. Scientific research was supported through Cassa finance, aiming to close the gap in research and development between the North and South.

By the 1970s, the Cassa was spending about 600 billion lire per annum. Figure 3 shows the proportionate breakdown of spending by the Cassa.

During the early 1980s, the Cassa was wound up, its functions absorbed by regional administration within the Mezzogiorno. However, in 1986, a new organisation was created, the Agency for the Promotion and Development of the Mezzogiorno. This took over the administration of regional incentive policy and the financing of regional development programmes.[18]

Comments and criticisms of the Cassa have focused on several issues. Supporters of the Cassa argue that considerable progress was made in the face of many difficult factors, such as the large size of the region, high unemployment, the original state of underdevelopment and the limited resources together with the late start of industrial development. Conspicuously good results were reported in agriculture and the provision of infrastructure.[19]

FIGURE 3

CASSA EXPENDITURE 1951–75[20]

Category	%
General infrastructure	22%
Agriculture	23%
Industry	27%
Tourism	2%
Other	26%
	100%

But critics of the Cassa argue that the per capita income gap between North and South has not narrowed, highlighting a number of difficulties. Commentators point to an excessive concentration of capital-intensive rather than labour-intensive enterprises. Some of these have been called 'cathedrals in the desert' i.e. giant manufacturing plants that are isolated from the local economy and thus fail to generate local employment. Critics argue that a diversified and self-generating industrial base was not created and that small and medium enterprises did not materialise.

A second criticism was about the proliferation of areas and nuclei, arguing that the principle of growth centres dictates a need to concentrate scarce resources in a limited number of areas. However, by the 1970s, forty-eight such areas and nuclei had been designated. This resulted in reduced selectivity and the spread of resources over a very wide geographical area. Related to this argument about excessive dispersal was the point that local development consortia multiplied to such an extent that practically the whole Mezzogiorno was covered. As a result, most consortia became completely dependent on the Cassa for funding – local initiative often meant, at best, initiative in requesting central aid.[21]

Highland and Islands Development Board

The Highlands and Islands of Scotland form a rugged, sparsely populated area, with a history of unemployment and population loss. The area stands apart from the rest of Britain in terms of poor access, mountainous terrain and a coastal fringe with numerous islands, such as the Hebrides, the Orkneys and the Shetland Isles.

Demands for special measures to develop the Highlands go back to the 1940s, and even earlier when an informal lobby group was established called the 'Highland Development League'. The League, comprising local leaders from the Highlands, agitated for government support for the area. During the 1960s, they were joined by the Scottish Trades Union Council in this pressure. In 1965, they were rewarded by a government decision to establish the Highlands and Islands Development Board (HIDB).

One writer has argued that there were political forces at play here:

> In 1965 the Labour government had a very slender majority, and there were nine liberals in the House of Commons, several of them representing Highland constituencies . . . all the legislation over the past century which has effectively changed the situation in the Highlands has been passed by governments clinging precariously to power.[22]

The legislation before the Houses of Parliament gave HIDB two main objectives: firstly, it was to assist the people of the Highlands and Islands to improve their economic and social conditions and, secondly, it was to enable the Highlands and Islands to play a more effective part in the economic and social development of the nation.[23] This Bill was particularly associated with the enthusiastic Secretary of State for Scotland, Willie Ross. Soon after the passage of the Bill, a discussion between Ross and the newly appointed Chairman of the HIDB agreed that an entirely new approach was needed for the development of the Highlands – one that was completely foreign to the previous practice of the Scottish Office.

It should be a new strategy, seen as being based in the Highlands, and risk-taking and adventurous. To match these objectives, the scope and range of HIDB activity would need to be especially wide.[24]

The initial plans for HIDB were largely determined by Bob Grieve, the founding Chairman. Grieve's vision was that the new Board should have headquarters in the Highlands. Major developments should be in forestry, tourism, fishing and industry, with related improvements in roads and transport. Grieve also believed that there should be a focus on two or three concentrations of population and industry, particularly associated with wood processing, maritime industry and offshore oil.

For major industrial development, HIDB supported a large scale pulp mill at Fort William and an aluminium smelter at Invergordon. These were to represent the 'industrial heartland' of the Highlands. However, both subsequently closed, and there was much controversy and criticism. Offshore oil development was considerable and a number of large platform construction yards were opened. Oil terminals transformed the local economy of some areas such as the Shetland Islands.

Sea fishing was supported by a number of measures including loans to young fishermen to buy new boats, training schemes to upgrade skills in the fishing industry and support for fish processing plants. Under these programmes, the number of fishing boats in the Highlands and Islands doubled between the 1960s and the 1980s.

Land reform was a further venture that came on the HIDB agenda. There were some instances where the presence of large estates curtailed development. This stimulated proposals to permit the Board to engage in compulsory purchase in these cases, acquiring the estates and breaking them up. But political support seems to have been lacking and the proposals came to nothing.

Tourism developments were encouraged by a number of programmes. Local tourist organisations were established, with grants and loans for new hotels and improvements to existing hotels. In some remote areas, HIDB built its own hotels.

For timber, HIDB concentrated on increasing added value through wood processing plants, and the development of a native Highland wood manufacture industry.

Local enterprise was supported through cooperative marketing programmes. Local community cooperatives were stimulated particularly in the Western Isles. Assistance was also given to improve community facilities in remoter areas. HIDB opened a network of twenty-four area offices to make itself more accessible to local communities.

In evaluating the HIDB, commentators have pointed to a number of positive outcomes from the agency's work. Firstly, the drift of population away from the Highlands has stopped. In 1971, for the first time in a century, population decline was halted. The population has increased since then. Secondly, the volume of projects supported has been substantial: in 1965–80, over 7,000 projects were given assistance of £80 million and created over 20,000 jobs. Thirdly, the gap in welfare between the Highlands and the rest of Britain has narrowed significantly. Unemployment in the Highlands was 8% in 1971 and 9% in 1980; for the whole of Britain, unemployment grew steeply, from 4% to 7% over the same period. Supporters of HIDB also argue that locating the agency within the Highlands made an important contribution to development:

> There is a geographical perspective which alters the appearance of problems as we view then in different environments.[25]

HIDB relied on community initiative rather than on individual initiative, and produced a variety of remedies to the wide range of development problems it faced.

However, critics of HIDB have pointed to a number of defects in the agency's approach. Some argue that HIDB had relatively little discretionary power and operated under the close control and scrutiny of the Scottish Office and allege that civil servants excessively narrowed the scope and range of HIDB activities. There have been arguments about local coordination and bureaucracy. Since HIDB was established in the 1960s, local government reform has been instituted, resulting in two regional councils in the agency's area – Highland Regional Council and Western Isles Council – both incorporating economic development functions. Questions have thus been asked about the role of HIDB, and duplication with the two councils. Similarly, overlap with the Scottish Development

Agency has also been noted. Finally, excessive reliance on the grants and supports of the HIDB have been criticised by some who have argued that the agency had fallen into the trap of being a simple grant-giver:

> we should not view the Board as it would like to be viewed, as a trusting, dynamic combination of research agency and action agency on the TVA model, but rather as a fairly passive milch cow.[26]

In 1991, HIDB was restructured into Highlands and Islands Enterprise (HIE), a new structure that combines the activities of HIDB with training and environmental roles, merging with the functions of the Training Agency. The new HIE is organised into ten Local Enterprise Companies, each locally based with private sector involvement to provide front-line delivery.

Congested Districts Board 1891–1923

The three development agencies we have looked at so far – the TVA, Cassa and HIDB – are late and middle twentieth-century organisations. There is, however, a nineteenth century precursor to these three. The Congested Districts Board (CDB) in the west of Ireland operated for a thirty-two year period, promoting development in a range of economic sectors in Ireland's western counties. At the time of its dissolution, a history of the CDB was written by its chief officer, W. Micks. This provided a rich insight into a unique regional programme in the early years of the twentieth century.[27]

The CDB was created by the Purchase of Land (Ireland) Act, 1891. At that time, Ireland was part of the United Kingdom, ruled from London by the Westminster Parliament. The preceding twenty years had been a time of social ferment and rural agitation with tenant unrest, boycotts of land-lords and political movements for home rule and revolutionary separatism. These threats were countered by the British government with social legislation, particularly in reform of land ownership.

The CDB was to be a development board for the 'congested districts' in the west of Ireland. These were rural areas with high density population, many living in conditions of extreme poverty and distress. Much of the momentum for establishing the CDB came from Arthur Balfour, the Chief Secretary for Ireland. In a memorandum at the foundation of the CDB, Balfour reported that the CDB would not be a government department in the ordinary sense, nor would it be subordinate to the Chief Secretary's office, nor to any minister. The CDB should be free to spend its income as it considered best, and to act directly or indirectly as it saw fit.

In his history of the CDB, Micks also confirmed this, claiming that wider powers could not have been given to the CDB, and that decisions made by the agency were final and unquestionable.

Under the 1891 Act, the CDB had a number of specific functions:

• To enable the purchase of small farms and the amalgamation and consolidation of small tenancies into larger holdings.
• To aid and develop agriculture, forestry, livestock and poultry, weaving and spinning, fishing and other suitable industries.

The area covered by the CDB included most western parts of the country. Finance for the new organisation was provided by a capital sum of £1.5 million, made available from the proceeds of the disestablishment and sales of property of the Protestant Church of Ireland – a measure also linked to the social reforms of the time.

Initial work in 1891 was to undertake a major survey of the social and economic conditions of the West of Ireland. Balfour particularly encouraged this, arguing in a memorandum that the mere elaboration of schemes, however excellent they might be, was not sufficient. In order that these schemes could be put into effective operation, some survey of the needs of the various districts was necessary, giving not only information about the problems, but also a baseline by which to calculate the exact amount of progress CDB was making. The result was completed one year later, a compendium of reports on eighty-four separate localities in the congested districts, providing a valuable statement of conditions in the areas involved.

Over the following three decades, the CDB undertook an extensive range of developments in agriculture, fisheries, industry and land reform. These took the following forms:

1. Agriculture: Instruction and advice through a network of local agricultural officers; improvement schemes for animal breeding and husbandry, particularly for horses, cattle, pigs, sheep and poultry; some tree planting, usually shelter-belts for farms.
2. Fisheries: Price and income supports for fishermen through the purchase by CDB of fish, in several specified locations, at fixed prices irrespective of volume bought; fish processing (pickling and drying); direct loans to fishermen for purchase and repair of boats; grants for construction of fishing piers.

3. Industry: Support for ideas and inventions to start new enterprises in products such as glass, bottles, pottery, paper, weaving and timber; loans for factories; local industry improvement schemes, operation of stores, inspection of markets, payment of price subsidies to local producers; operation of 'lace schools' to teach embroidery, lace making and knitting, with marketing of the products by the teachers.

4. Land purchase: The 1891 Act applied only to voluntary acquisition of tenants' property and a subsequent 1909 Act extended this to give CDB powers to acquire landlords' estates through compulsory purchase. Land was purchased and allocated to tenants and holdings were rearranged to maximise efficiencies; total acquisitions up to 1920 were 1,104 estates encompassing 2.6 million acres.

In his history of the organisation, Micks emphasised the need to build genuine economic schemes that would increase incomes at local level, not just relief works. He voiced sharp criticism of many of the public works programmes of his time. He saw them as fostering dependence:

> My personal experience of relief works has made me dislike them intensely . . . a desire of some shopkeepers and others to have money brought into and spent in a locality. If the promoters succeeded in their efforts almost every man in the district, whether in need or not, tried to get a share of what was going. It was a competition degrading to promoters and applicants.[28]

Micks was also scathing on what he saw as perpetual blockages placed in the organisation's way by the UK Treasury. He reported impositions of continuous delay by that body, so much so that, at one stage, the CDB actually instituted legal proceedings against the Treasury, a case that eventually found its way to the House of Lords where the decision was in favour of the CDB. Micks accused the Treasury of continuously blocking CDB proposals, usually with no knowledge of the case in question, with dogmatic opinions, one-sided statements, persistent use of veto and an air of sublime omniscience. He concluded that:

> when two or more bodies of *brainy* men have to agree on the details of any project great delay in its execution is sure to occur; or probably its complete abandonment may result.[29]

Micks argued that the moral behind the experience of the CDB was that bodies charged with the development of the resources of the country should be given a wide and unfettered discretion. He claimed that opportunities would pass away if every idea or project had to run the gauntlet of outside officials who did not possess the special knowledge required.

In spite of the problems with the Treasury the CDB did enjoy a large measure of independence, with the credit for this laid firmly by Micks with Arthur Balfour, the Chief Secretary for Ireland. According to Micks, Balfour took the strong view that outside official interference should be minimised, a policy that granted much discretion and freedom.

The formation of the Irish Free State, and the creation of a national government in Dublin, spelled the end of the CDB, according to Micks. He wrote that the CDB had been established because there was no confidence in Ireland in 1891 in the ability of the British Government to remedy the deplorable conditions of the inhabitants in the congested districts. As soon as an independent Irish government was established, the reason for the continuance of the CDB ceased to exist, according to Micks. However, the abolition of the CDB was also influenced by other forces. The CDB was seen by central government officials in the new administration as outside the regular method of operation of the civil service, an independent body not answerable to the new Irish parliament. This factor generated considerable criticism of the organisation.[30] Consequently, the functions of the CDB were transferred to several different departments of the new government in 1923, and the organisation was disbanded.

Viewed from the standpoint of the 1990s, the CDB has drawn some very favourable comment. The CDB was reported to be highly innovative – in its socio-economic planning, in its regional emphasis, and in its inclusive non party-political composition. In effect, the CDB became the earliest clear example of rural regional planning in Europe.[31]

This review of a number of development agencies identifies several significant features and distinguishing characteristics:

- They are geographically focused, based on a defined locality with specific needs and potential.
- They are multipurpose in scope and active in several economic sectors, with emphasis on different sectors shifting over time.
- They report directly to central government (in the case of the agencies here) and are therefore closely associated with national political developments.
- Their relationships with local groups attract considerable attention: the form of this relationship is not universally defined and varies between agencies.

• At the start-up phase, the influence of individual personalities and leaders is significant.

Overall, the stories of the agencies demonstrate several common themes and issues, providing a useful framework for the investigation of the SFADCo case study.

TWO

The Two Paradigms of Regional Development

R EGIONAL development has been an issue attracting academic attention since the 1950s. The basic definitions and nomenclature were laid down in the 1960s.

Regional development has been defined as the where of economic development – once governments talk about a spatial dimension to national policy, we enter the realm of regional development.[1] Proponents of regional development policies have pointed to both economic and social arguments to support their case. Economically, regional policies reduce the costs of congestion in core urban areas, and exploit underutilised resources in underdeveloped areas; socially, regional policies integrate a society and promote equity.[2]

Friedmann[3] claimed that problems of regional imbalance were greatest in countries at a transitional stage of their development, where the income gap between core and periphery became steadily wider. The issue of core and periphery was central to regional development, with a relationship between the two types of region that was essentially 'colonial'. Factors of production, labour, capital and entrepreneurship become displaced from the periphery to the core. The periphery remains a producer of primary goods and terms of trade are favourable to the core. The core regions monopolise higher value activities, such as manufacturing.

Friedmann set out a number of propositions for regional development theory:

- Regional economies are subject to external influence and regional growth is externally induced.
- Export growth needs to be translated into growth of the local sectors, but this depends on the socio-political structure of the region.
- Local leadership is decisive for adaptation to change: the quality of leadership depends on the region's past experience with development.
- Regional economic growth may be regarded as a problem in the location of firms, and occurs in a matrix of urban regions.

- Where economic growth is sustained over long periods, there is a decline in regional disparities and a progressive integration of the space economy.

Friedmann also identified a series of five regional types.

1. Core regions: These are characterised by their high promise for economic growth, consisting of one or more clustered cities. Their problems are how to sustain growth, manage congestion, absorb incoming population, organise the physical environment and cope with conflicting demands for space.
2. Upward transitional regions: These are areas of in-migration with the possibility of a greatly intensified use of natural resources. They encompass urban and rural areas. Their problems are associated with rapid economic growth, agricultural adjustment, urbanisation and industrial development. Development corridors between core regions are typical upward transitional areas.
3. Downward transitional regions: These are old and established regions with a stagnant or declining economic base due to several factors such as urban obsolescence or contraction of a dominant sector. A downward transitional region could be rural with declining agricultural employment, or urban with cutbacks in industrial sectors such as steel or textiles, or an area affected by the closure of coal mines.
4. Resource frontiers: These are zones of new settlement in virgin territories and areas of new population whose problems include isolation, weak supply lines and absence of infrastructure.
5. Special problem regions: These are areas with a peculiar set of resource or locational factors, such as river valleys, border regions and special tourism zones.

Friedmann's view was that problems of regional development could not be viewed in isolation. A partial solution to difficulties in one region may be found in action in another region, emphasising complementary and inter-related approaches. Friedmann argued that regional development policies in resource frontier and downward transitional regions needed to follow certain principles:

- Some measure of regional authority or sovereignty was necessary, with community leadership as a central issue.

- Development needed to have an urban focus to develop towns to a critical size and designate growth points with central services.
- Access and reduction of isolation were critical, with the emphasis on transport networks.
- The economic base needed to be diversified.
- Knowledge centres, such as a regional university, needed to be established.

A critical strategy for regional development, according to Friedmann, was the nature of the regional approach, a solution different from the national approach:

> The regional approach to development differs radically from sectoral planning. Its purpose is to achieve an integration of individual sector programs for the solution of problem complexes on a regional scale.[4]

Policies towards regional development have followed a number of streams of thought and sets of ideas. They can be summed up by two distinctive schools of thought – 'development from above' or 'development from below'. These can be described as 'paradigms' within the field of regional development – statements of the core meanings of particular issues, representing alternative models, theories or frameworks (paradigms are central concepts or policy directions). The value of classifying ideas according to the paradigm to which they belong is that we can see more clearly the themes and patterns of diverse thinking within the subject.

THE FIRST PARADIGM: DEVELOPMENT FROM ABOVE

Initial thinking in regional development highlighted the need for 'balanced' development, or an adequate 'spread' of investment. But all this was challenged by Perroux who argued that balanced development was a myth:

> The bitter truth is this: growth does not appear everywhere at the same time: it becomes manifest at points or poles of growth, with variable intensity; it spreads through different channels, with variable terminal effects on the whole of the economy.[5]

Perroux thus advanced the idea of the 'growth pole' – a motor or key industry whose growth has a propulsive effect on the entire regional economy. Other industries are stimulated, industry clusters emerge, the collective needs of new investment are satisfied and an industrial tradition develops.

For Perroux, the key industry was an industry whose increase in output had the effect of generating still further increases in output in other sectors (the 'affected' industries). The key industry thus had high growth rates, high levels of development with factors of production separated from each other, high levels of specialisation, division of labour and significant concentrations of capital. The effect of the key industry is to set in motion a set of dynamic impulses throughout the regional economy: expectations are raised, innovations are stimulated and additional income is created and diffused. Perroux emphasised that an entire sector could display innovative characteristics, highlighting that innovation was not thus simply a matter for individual entrepreneurs.

A cluster of industries develops, consisting of the interaction of the key industry and affected industries, emerging in a geographically agglomerated industrial 'pole' or growth centre. Here there is an intensification of economic activities because of proximity and human contacts which produce consumers whose consumption patterns are diversified and progressive compared to rural agricultural environments. Collective needs such as housing and transport emerge. Because of agglomeration, these needs can be met in a more economic way than if they appeared in a dispersed pattern. Furthermore, new types of producers appear, such as entrepreneurs and skilled workers, each influencing the other and forging a new industrial tradition. Perroux's idea of the growth pole thus provided the rationale and justification for policies of growth centres in regional development.

The relationship between the growth centre and the surrounding periphery has been discussed by a number of writers. Hirschmann argued that an economy must develop one or several regional centres of economic strength to lift itself to higher income levels, emphasising a need for the emergence of 'growing points' or 'growth poles'.[6] The consequence is, therefore, that inequality of growth is a necessary part of the development process and that growth is necessarily unbalanced. There are, however, a number of mechanisms that promote the transmission of growth from the growth points to lagging regions.

This transmission of growth is called 'trickle down'. Growth in one area can have favourable effects on other areas through the trickle down process: demand for products in the lagging regions is stimulated – investment spreads from the growth point to other areas. Thus while growth is necessarily unbalanced, a trickle down effect takes place where the benefits of growth spread from the centre to other areas. Trade, investment and government policies are all mechanisms through which this trickle down effect can be secured.

Hirschmann also acknowledged that there were countervailing negative forces at work: growth points compete against lagging regions and suppress development there, a consequence called 'polarisation'. However, Hirschmann believed that the longer term effect was for the trickle down process to outweigh the polarisation effect.

THE SECOND PARADIGM: DEVELOPMENT FROM BELOW

During the 1970s, confidence in formal regional development programmes, particularly dependent on inward investment, waned considerably. There were a number of reasons for this. Firstly, many types of development came to be seen as creating greater dependence of the periphery on the core regions and maintaining reliance by the poor regions on rich regions. Many forms of development reinforced the established competitive advantage of strong regions over weak regions. Secondly, many forms of development aggravated the problem of the 'dual economy' with valuable employment in 'traditional' labour intensive sectors threatened by the social and economic changes of 'modernisation'. Thirdly, the trickle down or 'spread' effect of growth centres was not perceived as working. In practice, growth centres were seen by some to be costly and expensive, generating still further inequalities and depressing initiative in developing regions.

An early precursor of this thinking was Myrdal who claimed that circular and cumulative causation worked in a vicious circle to reinforce inequalities between rich and poor regions.[7] Even an accidental factor, such as a factory closure, can set in motion a stream of events. The closure results in lower local incomes, a reduced tax base in the area and falling standards of services and infrastructure that weaken the prospect of other development. Similarly, the same cumulative process works in a favourable situation as the location of a new industry gives a spur to general development with higher incomes, greater skills, spin-off businesses and strengthened local tax base. Myrdal thus concluded that market forces work towards inequality. If matters were left to market forces unhampered by policy interventions, almost all those economic activities in a developing economy that give a greater than average rate of return would cluster in certain localities, leaving the rest of the country more or less in a backwater. The result is that growth in the strong centres generates a 'backwash' effect. Resources such as capital and skills are sucked into the centre from peripheral areas: migration from poor to rich areas is selective, drawing skills out of weaker communities and increased demand in strong centres siphons off savings in the weak region. The freeing of markets confers competitive advantage in trade on the growth centres. Weaker regions thus found themselves in progressively more dependent relationships with the strong growth points.

Seers pointed to the need for self-reliant development to reduce dependence, arguing that economic growth cannot be equated with development.[8] Growth could, in fact, be damaging unless issues like inequality, unemployment and poverty were declining. He claimed that 'development' should imply reducing cultural dependence on the great powers, and adopting a selective approach to external influences. Seers argued for self-reliance in development strategies, such as reduced dependence on imports, redistribution of income and an improved capacity for negotiation. He highlighted four particular targets for self-reliant development:

1. Ownership as well as output in the leading economic sectors: issues of redistribution, social progress and political change are central to the meaning of 'development'.
2. Consumption patterns that economise on foreign exchange: forms of development that limit demand for foreign consumer goods and reduce dependence on imports should be at a premium.
3. Institutional capacity for research and negotiation, particularly negotiation with foreign governments and transnational corporations.
4. Cultural goals appropriate to the area: as cultural factors shape the way people perceive their material needs, development must be appropriate to the culture, values and lifestyle of the people affected.

Stohr has argued that development should be 'from below' rather than 'from above' and claims that there is a 'centre-down' development paradigm i.e. a set of implicit ideas about development from above.[9] These ideas contain a number of erroneous assumptions:

• Development should be by the select few.
• Others are incapable of taking initiative.
• Development leaders are willing to allow others to participate.
• Modern development should replace traditional development.

Stohr argued for an alternative paradigm for development – development from below – an alternative approach to create development impulses and generate growth from within the region concerned. The objectives of development should be to mobilise natural, human and institutional resources, incorporating a number of key ingredients in effective development strategies:

- Opening access to land.
- Organising decision-making and self-determination territorially.
- Using appropriate technology.
- Meeting basic needs.
- Using managed pricing policies.
- Allowing some limited external assistance.
- Focusing on action to increase living standards.
- Restructuring transport systems.
- Developing collective consciousness and cooperation.

Stohr has also claimed that fundamental changes have come about in the direction of regional policy. Traditional policies tended to focus on issues of quantitative growth, with centralised organisation based on large investments of capital in a limited number of growth centres. This has given way to a different approach emphasising regional innovation, decentralisation, mobilisation of local resources and large volumes of small projects. This view of Stohr is summarised in Figure 4 following.

However, the development from below approach has attracted significant criticism, with a number of arguments highlighting its weaknesses.[11] These issues are listed here:

- The development from below proponents have been accused of being utopian, seeking too much and being unwilling to accept incremental changes in development programmes.
- They were antagonistic to all other forms of development and did not lend themselves well to the consensus-building essential for policy innovation.
- They rejected too heartily the role of the state and large organisations, thereby distancing themselves from important institutional structures that could be helpful.
- Local autonomy sometimes created more problems than solutions, giving rise to creating significant difficulties for coordination and management.
- There is little hard evidence that development from below can secure real economic growth.

Arguments such as these suggest that the last word has not been said, and that significant potential exists for the further development of ideas in this field.

FIGURE 4

CHANGES IN REGIONAL POLICY: SOME CHARACTERISTICS[10]

Characteristic	Traditional policy	Future policy
Problem regions	dichotomous (underdeveloped/ developed)	multifaceted (different regional structural weaknesses)
Major strategy	regional growth	regional innovation
Major organisation	centralised, state-sponsored	decentralised, regional and community-based
Dominant mechanism	inter-regional distribution	mobilisation of indigenous regional resources
Major orientation	capital, material	information, technology, intangibles
	growth (quantitative)	flexibility (qualitative)
	manufacturing	services and intersectoral linkages
	projects	programmes
	few large firms projects	numerous small
Dynamics	geographically 'stable' problem regions	rapidly shifting (elusive) problem areas
	fixed set of 'planned' growth centres	spontaneous local resource mobilisation

THREE

Organisational Aspects

I N THIS chapter we will look at the institutional aspects of regional development i.e. the regional agencies and how they work in a social and human dimension, an approach that puts organisational factors to the fore. A number of aspects are of particular significance here.[1]

WITHIN THE ORGANISATION

Within the organisation there are several dynamics going on, a number of which are of specific interest.

- Learning and unlearning.
- Entrepreneurship.
- Managerial innovation.
- Leadership and authority.
- Ideologies and values.

Learning and unlearning

The issue of how organisations adapt to changing circumstances is a significant question. Organisations learn and unlearn as they travel through different environments and time periods and learning is part of the response of the organisation to the external world. Learning can do several things: it can be cumulative, adding to lessons learnt in previous periods – a continuous process. Alternatively, learning can be discontinuous, representing once-off additions to the stock of knowledge in an organisation. Learning can have negative consequences: it can enslave and restrict. However, it can also liberate and develop the organisation, helping the agency to change the environment around it.

Learning is a process whereby organisations assemble stimuli to the external environment, selecting some and rejecting others, depending on their perception. Organisations need to learn at different levels, such as:

- Adjustment learning: minor changes, relatively easy.
- Turnover learning: significant change, requires unlearning and development of new behaviour.
- Turnaround learning: Substantial change requiring new principles and theories.

Adjustment learning is going on all the time, but turnover or turnaround learning require strategic change.

Organisational learning is triggered by several mechanisms, most commonly problems. Gaps between performance and expectation may cause organisations to search for new approaches. Opportunities are a second type of trigger, with organisational learning stimulated by the perception of new possibilities. The third trigger is people: individual members of the organisation, such as leaders, managers and others can initiate new knowledge into the structure.

Unlearning is the process by which organisations discard knowledge. Organisations unlearn by changing their old behaviour and theories for new ones, a typically problem-triggered process. Financial shortages, diminishing popular support and external criticism are factors that cause hesitancy and build up distrust in established procedures and methods. These previous strategies are then unlearnt in favour of new ones. A balance needs to be established between an organisation's abilities to learn and unlearn.

Organisations can increase their ability to learn and unlearn by a number of means, such as experimentation and exploration, awareness of external stimuli, providing a rewarding environment for risk taking and creating balance and tension between different viewpoints.

For development agencies, the question is how do they learn? What are the mechanisms by which learning and unlearning occur? Development agencies are by definition agents of change: what are the implications of learning and unlearning in that process?[2]

Entrepreneurship

The issue of integrating the entrepreneur into the organisation has attracted significant attention, highlighted by the theme of entrepreneurship i.e. the process that involves the novel combination of factors of production. The emphasis is thus on entrepreneurship as a process, rather than the entrepreneur as a person. Entrepreneurship can be displayed by people who are within organisations and so is not necessarily restricted to the self-employed.

Entrepreneurship can thus be 'built in' to organisations. Entrepreneurial organisations display distinctive characteristics: they are frequently found in newly-developing industries, they have a single mission clearly understood by all their members and they have a fluid, goal-oriented structure without formalisation.

Managerial innovation

The ability of managers to innovate ensures the adaptability of their organisations. An innovation needs to be adopted by the organisation and the rate of adoption is influenced by several factors e.g. characteristics of administrators, size of organisation, structure, relationship with other organisations and competition.

Diffusion refers to the spread of an innovation to potential adopters and is influenced by internal networks within the organisation e.g. word of mouth, face-to-face contact. There are 'brokers' of innovations, who mediate between the potential user and the originator of the innovation. Organisations adopting innovation are seen by researchers as responsive to changing environments. In many cases, it is individuals, not organisations, that adopt. The perception and acceptance of innovations is very much influenced by individuals within organisations. In other cases the organisation is the crucial vehicle for adoption of an innovation.

Organisational adaptability is influenced by innovation and organisations adopt innovations to adjust to their environment. But innovation does not equal adaptability. Organisations must be able to distinguish between strategic and important innovations, and operational innovations. They must also be able to dispose of old innovations.

The issues of entrepreneurship and innovation are central to development agencies. How do development agencies promote these processes, both internally and externally? What are the blockages? How can entrepreneurship and innovation be stimulated and managed? The answer is through good leadership.

Leadership and authority

All organisations seek to control their members through the exercise of power and authority, a control secured by a number of means, particularly material and symbolic. Material controls are represented by economic payment of goods and services. Symbolic controls are those which arise through the exercise of leadership, particularly leadership that appeals to interpersonal relationships and social values.

Authority is derived from leadership. This leadership may be through formal or informal means, or both. Formal leadership flows from official position in an organisation while informal leadership is built on the attitudes and expectations of the participants.

In the development context, the question is about the relative significance of personal leadership. Is leadership a real issue in regional development, or is development instead all about policies, strategies and procedures?[3]

Ideologies and values

Organisations exist in a wider social context that bestows a framework of ideologies and values – general ideas that link goals to specific actions. Ideologies have a number of functions for organisations, both providing solidarity for the members and binding them together, and also rationalising the actions of the agency, thus granting it legitimacy.

Ideologies flow from national culture. The setting of the wider society generates the prevailing assumptions and justifications for what the organisation is doing. This creates general patterns of values that underpin the agency's actions. These values contain cultural ideas about property, wealth, work, enterprise, education and other dimensions. These ideas both constrain the organisation from some actions, and encourage it towards others. Ideologies also arise within organisations. They are the central ideas and values that explain the agency. Every organisation has its 'myths' i.e. the history, stories and legends of the organisation that legitimate its existence and provide strong motivation for the members.

For development agencies, the issue is about the culture of development. What ideological considerations influence development decisions? How do cultural values intervene in the development process? How does these ideologies and values change over time?

IMPLICATIONS OF THE EXTERNAL SOCIAL ENVIRONMENT

The wider social environment is mediated by the organisation through a variety of mechanisms, namely:

- Laws and rules.
- Class and power.
- Interdependence.
- Networks.

- Competition.
- Relating to the public.

We will look at these in turn.

Laws and rules

Organisations adapt to law enforcement and the imposition of rules and regulations imposed by the wider society. The relationship between organisations and rules is highly complex. At one level organisations respond to laws and rules, reflecting a 'compliance' model. The law is the stimulus and the agency responds by conforming to that stimulus. But the evidence is that a view of such conformity is too simplistic. Organisations are also non-compliant. They may try to evade the law, or interpret it in particular ways that promote their objectives, devising their own rules and adapting the application of law to that. There are thus two extremes of absolute compliance and absolute non-compliance. Both extremes are somewhat unreal, with many organisations responding to the pressures of the law some way between the two polar opposites.

There is another way of looking at organisations and the law. The organisation could be the independent stimulus, and the law the dependent response, with the organisation influencing how the law is made, and what law is made. The organisation is viewed as a lobbyist seeking to influence other groups for its own objectives – groups such as the government, political decision-makers, the judiciary and the police – with the focus on how it manipulates the legal environment for its own ends, rather than just responding to that environment.

Development agencies operate within a legal environment of powers and controls. How do agencies seek to influence that environment? Political lobbying? Administrative liaison? Are they passive recipients of legislative measures, or do they actively try to influence the outcome of law-making? We must look at the issue of class and power to find the answer.

Class and power

Societies are stratified in terms of power, wealth and prestige. Organisations reflect this and the way in which formal organisations are exploited by ruling élites is a significant issue. The impact of social class depends on the type of society – whether it is dominated by 'pluralist' or 'monolithic' qualities. All societies display at least some characteristics of both.

A pluralistic society has many diverse interests and pressure groups as several power groups may compete for resources. Membership of ruling groups may be available to many and clients may be strong enough to exert demands on the organisation, spawning competing forces. The organisation will act in a type of 'marketplace', facing rival demands made on it and under pressure to reconcile choices between these alternatives.

By contrast, a monolithic society is one where the rulers control both the resources needed by organisations as well as the demands of clients for the services of the organisation. In this case the organisations will be sponsored by particular rulers, with the organisational hierarchy dictated by the rulers and the organisational policies set by the rulers' agenda.

With development agencies, the question is how do they relate to the ruling groups in a society? Are development agencies dominated by a narrow range of influential people, or are they instead responding to a wide variety of interests and pressures?[4]

Interdependence

Some organisations evolve with heavy interdependence on others whereas some seek to maintain a centralised and independent existence. Interdependence is frequently a method of organisational adaptability. How does this evolution come about? What makes an organisation adopt a stance of interdependence rather than independence?

Factors that encourage interdependence include technology, resource use, responses of clients, social and political issues and others. In some cases the impetus to interdependence comes from a prime mover, such as a single cause or individual. In other cases it arises from an interaction of several factors. Organisations that embrace interdependence tend to be 'polycentric' i.e. they have a diffused distribution of power, and are internally diverse, focusing on the creation of networks with external actors. Organisations that emphasise independence are often centralised in structure with uniform patterns of activity.

Do development agencies positively forge alliances of interdependence with others, or do they seek to maintain an independent existence? This is influenced by networks.

Networks

Related to the interdependence issue is the matter of networks. Organisations operate in an environment of networks – systems of ties and connections between organisations. These links are of several types: they may consist of an exchange of resources or information; they may be hierarchical, implying control or ownership, or they may represent alliances, temporary or permanent, for joint action.

Networks can be stable and endure over a period of time or they can be unstable, subject to incessant change. Networks have important functions for organisations: they allow for sharing of power and resources; they provide for personnel flows between organisation and they facilitate diffusion of innovation. Networks offer significant conflict-management functions to mediate relationships between organisations.

Competition

Organisations compete against each other, irrespective of what sector they are in, or whether they are in the public or private domain. A series of factors dictate the degree of rivalry and competition.

Firstly, the number of organisations is a significant variable influencing rivalry. The greater the number, the less opportunity exists for any one operator to influence the outcome: coordination or cartels between operators are more difficult with large numbers. Secondly, the degree of equality between organisations is important; equal sizes of market share or funds induce competition – there is no natural leader to dominate the group. Thirdly, heterogeneity of value systems promotes competition. Where organisations share a common culture with homogeneous expectations, there is likely to be a greater degree of cooperation between them, such as a management class with a common lifestyle. In contrast, where there are strong variations in attitudes and between people in different organisations, competition and rivalry are encouraged.

The efficiency of outside pressure groups is also a critical factor. Where trade unions, clients and suppliers are well organised and effective, the scope for collaboration between operators in a sector will be limited. A sophisticated and informed clientele is an example of this. In contrast, where other groups are not well organised, or are weak, the potential for cooperation between operators is greater, and competition is less.

Development agencies do compete. Certainly, when they represent different regions or countries, competition between them is an expression of regional or national rivalries. Within a single country is there competition between agencies? What is the significance of this competition?

Relating to the public

Organisations need to pay close attention to the changing expectations of the public, selecting sections and regulating relationships with them. Organisations have to ensure that routine interaction with the public generates information about ways to improve performance. Through this information flow, organisations learn and adjust their approach to their public. Strategies towards involvement of the organisation's public are central to this, particularly involvement of employees, consumers or clients. Frequently, proposals within the organisation for new client or consumer involvement require cultural or social change for the agency itself.[5]

Development agencies face different sections of the public: employers, employees, investors, citizens and others. How do they manage relationships with these public groups with whom they interact?

THEMES FOR INVESTIGATION

This review of administrative aspects, together with the agency profile and the summary of the field of regional development, provides a basis for suggested themes for investigation and indicates some key issues about agencies in local and regional development. Three themes emerge:

- Leaders and personalities.
- Goals and visions.
- Relationships with other groups: local and national.

Leaders and personalities

What is the role of individuals in development? The literature suggests that change is frequently dependent on the driving energies of particular individuals, champions or leaders. Do these individuals really exert a tangible influence, or do they simply act as implementors of public policy? How do personalities effect the creation and outcome of development policy?

The proponents of the 'development from below' theory highlight the vital role they believe is played by local leaders, activists, animators and initiators. The experience of the development agencies does indeed indicate the impact of particular personalities: the original legislation for the Cassa per il Mezzogiorno was especially promoted by Mr De Gasferi, the head of the Italian government; the development of TVA was heavily influenced by its chairman, David Lilienthal; the foundation and direction of HIDB in Scotland was led by the Secretary of State for Scotland, Willie Ross and the first chairman, Bob Grieve; Arthur Balfour, the Chief Secretary for Ireland, gave considerable personal direction to the Congested Districts Board.

Goals and visions

How organisations define their goals has a critical impact on the strategies they follow, and on the outcome and impact of their work. But how are goals defined? What processes go into the activity of goal formation? Are goals general and visionary, or specific and operational, or both? What are the implications of different types of goals?

All four agencies were driven by strong visions, often associated with particular individuals. The Cassa was to establish a programme for Southern Italy based on consistent policies, taking account of economic and social needs. There was an emphasis on innovation and it originally carried out special tasks and extraordinary interventions. The TVA was imbued with the visions of President Roosevelt. At the time of the 1933 legislation, he called for a project in the service of the people that gave life to all forms of human concerns – a government corporation with the flexibility and initiative of private enterprise that marked a return to the spirit and vision of the pioneer. Similarly, the formation of HIDB was affected by visions of creativity, local initiative and progressive development. The Congested Districts Board was also powered by visions of local initiative, significant for the nineteenth century.

Certainly such visions were a motivating power in establishing the organisations. The literature has also confirmed the role of goals and visions. Dudley Seers[6] pointed to the need for cultural goals in development, while Walter Stohr[7] has emphasised the qualitative aspects involved. But do these visions last? How do they become operationalised in terms of action? How do visions impact on decision-making?

Relationships with other groups: local and national

Organisational literature is heavily imbued with the concept of 'network': how organisations cooperate with other entities, forging alliances and partnerships. The issue of these relationships arises on a number of levels, such as local and national.

The literature on regional development has focused, in many cases, on the local aspects of development and the role of community groups. For example, John Friedmann highlights the issue of regional sovereignty as a mechanism in development;[8] Dudley Seers has pointed to the need for self-reliant development;[9] Walter Stohr argues for development from below with territorially organised decision-making, self-determination and local resource mobilisation.[10]

Concern for local involvement has also been central to much of the consciousness of the development agencies themselves. TVA claimed to be founded very much on the principles of decentralised administration, people participation and social responsibility, all within the context of a 'grass roots' approach. The Cassa sought to promote local involvement through development Consortia at district level that involved public representatives, chambers of commerce and others. The HIDB established an extensive network of local area offices and community cooperatives. The Congested Districts Board displayed a strong local presence.

Agencies relate to local groups but use alternative approaches to community participation, and these approaches vary over time. Consultation with economic and social interests has recently been studied by Coombes et al.[11] They claimed that there are a number of different approaches to consultation:

- Functional representation: Part of normal administrative machinery.
- Concertation: Permanent collaboration and consensus building on an informal basis.
- Co-optation: Absorbing other groups as a means of averting threats.
- Social partnership: Formal collaboration with interest groups.
- Interdependence: Management of interorganisational networks.

Each of these five approaches is used by development agencies, but different approaches are favoured and used under different conditions with varying consequences. At the national level, relationships must be handled with central administration and tensions must be managed. In the case of TVA, the observation was made that the authority distanced itself from national federal administration, thereby weakening its voice. In the case of HIDB, arguments have been made about heavy-handed control from the Scottish Office.

From a national perspective, there may be latent political goals served by the agencies with informal political consequences. TVA was recognised to be a forerunner of Roosevelt's 'new deal' policies. The Cassa was part of a Christian Democrat approach to deny the Italian Communist Party victories at the ballot box. The HIDB's establishment may have been influenced by the relationship between the Scottish Liberals and the Labour Party. The formation of the CDB was an intrinsic part of the social reforms of ninetenth century Ireland. Such political aspects may affect the operation of the agencies, or they may be purely incidental or background.

External relationships help organisations to learn and unlearn, the literature on the development agencies providing many examples of policy change and adaptation. TVA adjusted its approach to power generation on several occasions; the Cassa changed emphasis from agricultural to industrial policies. Organisations assemble responses to the external environment through the selection of stimuli in the environment. How they select these stimuli and respond to them is worthy of discussion. They interpret the stimuli, and this interpretation is affected by the external network of relationships.

These three issues of the history of the agencies, the paradigms of development and the organisational aspects thus set the framework for the case study of the Shannon story. The framework has provided us with a set of ideas and general principles to inform the case study. To this story we now turn.

II

The Case Study of Shannon Free Airport Development Company

FOUR

Establishment of the Company[1]

NATIONAL CONTEXT

THE ESTABLISHMENT of SFADCo was very much a part of the intensive structural changes that Ireland was undergoing at that time – changes that defined the economic and political forces shaping the agency.

In the early 1940s, Irish economic policy was influenced heavily by economic nationalism, expressed in an elaborate system of restraints such as import quotas, tariff protection for domestic industry and statutory limitations on investment by foreigners within the country (the 'Control of Manufactures' legislation). The emphasis was on development of native enterprise through native resources, although during the 1950s this policy came to be progressively abandoned as it was seen to be inadequate. Ireland experienced an economic crisis of gigantic proportions: between 1951 and 1961, 400,000 emigrants left Ireland; there were severe problems with the balance of payments; gross national product was stagnant; rural depopulation accelerated, and manufacturing output declined.

From the early 1950s, government thinking moved towards the idea of attracting foreign capital with the initial impetus for this coming from the postwar Marshall Plan. During the 1940s, Ireland had received almost £150m in Marshall aid. In order to make the case for American aid, a recovery programme had to be outlined, with plans and projections. This encouraged greater thinking about internationalisation, and led to an increased focus on productivity and output. By 1955, economic expansion with foreign investment was becoming the accepted wisdom among many parties. In 1954–57 the then coalition government introduced export tax incentives and opened the question of Ireland's admission to the International Monetary Fund and the World Bank.

In 1958, the Secretary of the Department of Finance, Mr Whitaker, published a paper entitled *Economic Development*. This paper had a profound effect on Irish economic policy. It argued that one of the biggest problems was to reshape public capital expenditure so that it would provide productive and self-sustaining employment. Funds were to be directed into state aid for marketing and research, land improvements, development of new industry, fishery and tourism with the main source of finance to be a cutback in social or 'non-productive' expenditure. Whitaker advocated an integrated development programme to staunch the flow of emigration and attract foreign capital. Only profitable sectors of the economy were to be boosted, stressing entrepreneurship and productive rather than social investment. Subsidies for inefficient sectors were to be reduced and tax incentives were to be offered to exporting industry.[2]

The paper on economic development was incorporated into the *First Programme for Economic Expansion* which was published later in 1958 and followed by a series of subsequent programmes. This heralded a period of fresh thinking and new approaches, illustrated by the following schedule of publications and key events:

> 1958 *Economic Development* report
> 1959 *First Programme for Economic Expansion*
> 1961 Committee on Industrial Organisation established by government
> 1961 Ireland applies for EEC membership
> 1963 *Second Programme for Economic Expansion*
> 1963 National Industrial and Economic Council established
> 1965 Anglo–Irish Free Trade Agreement

The first Whitaker paper on economic development had been prepared during the period of the coalition government (1954–57) and much of the new thinking emerged at that time. The subsequent government under the Fianna Fáil party came from a background of economic nationalism and strong republicanism. Sean Lemass was Minister for Industry and Commerce in 1957. He later became Prime Minister (Taoiseach) in 1959. But Lemass continued the momentum of outward-looking policies by promoting the emerging programmes with his own particular verve and dynamism:

> Lemass, if not quite the superman claimed by devotees of his brand of economic expansionism, was a tough-minded meritocrat, energetic and unsentimental to a refreshing degree.[3]

Lemass's objective was to secure a shift in policy from agricultural subsidies and tariff protection in another direction – towards free trade, expansion of exports and incentives to inward investment. In doing this, he had to contend with several pressure groups and interest groups in Irish society at the time. Some republicans and nationalists were suspicious of the shift to free trade, a number of Irish industries already under protection sought continuation of the tariffs that shielded them and farming interests argued for the importance of their sector. Consequently, with these constraints and traps, Lemass was enthusiastic to see emerging in Shannon a movement that typified and symbolised the policies he was spearheading. This was the economic and political context that supported the emergence of SFADCo.

BACKGROUND

In October 1957, Sean Lemass, Minister for Industry and Commerce, submitted a proposal to a cabinet meeting of the Irish government. The proposal was that the Comptroller of Sales and Catering at Shannon Airport should be given wider functions to include the development of traffic, tourism and airfreight. The activity would be financed out of Sales and Catering revenue, although a start-up allocation of £50,000 would be made by the government. This so-called allocation was in fact permission to retain profits that would otherwise have been handed back to government. The cabinet agreement to this proposal laid the basis for the ultimate creation of Shannon Free Airport Development Company Ltd – SFADCo.

Milestones leading up to the 1957 decision can be summarised as follows:

1935 Landing sites selected at Shannon Airport for both land-based aircraft and flying boats.

1937 First flying boat lands at Foynes on the southern bank of the Shannon Estuary, opposite the proposed airport site.

1939 First scheduled transatlantic flight into Foynes and first land-based aircraft (Douglas DC4) begin operations at Shannon Airport.

1943 Brendan O'Regan appointed catering controller at Foynes.

1945 Aviation and catering operations transferred to Shannon Airport.

1947 Shannon designated as world's first 'Customs Free Airport'

1957 Shannon Free Airport Development Company Ltd established.

The origins of SFADCo lay in the establishment of Shannon Airport, first mooted in 1935. Development of the airport was motivated by Ireland's strategic value as a starting and finishing point for flights between Europe and North America. This was dictated by limits of payload and freight. Initial aviation developed just before World War II. Passengers travelled by flying boat from North America to Foynes, County Limerick. They were then transferred by coach to Shannon Airport (then called Rineanna) for onward connection by land plane to the South of England. At that time, flying boats were seen as the future of transatlantic aviation.

This type of operation inevitably generated a strong demand for catering facilities. To meet this need, a catering comptroller, Brendan O'Regan, was appointed in 1943.

BRENDAN O'REGAN[4]

Brendan O'Regan's background gave him many elements that were of value in the task. He was born in County Clare. His father was a prominent local hotelier as well as chairman of Clare County Council (a member of the then opposition party, Fine Gael), placing O'Regan in a strong social position in the political and commercial life of the area. His early experience in helping to manage the Ennis Old Ground Hotel with his father had been supplemented by overseas training in London, Germany and Switzerland. This type of foreign exposure in the pre-war years made the young O'Regan very much an exception in the Irish hotel industry. On his return to Ireland, O'Regan managed his father's second hotel, the Falls Hotel in Ennistymon, Co. Clare.

It was in the Falls Hotel that O'Regan first came into contact with a network that was to provide him with major opportunities in the years ahead. During the early war years, senior civil servants from Dublin used to patronise the Falls Hotel. They were impressed with the verve and energy of the young owner-manager. About the same time, the very prestigious St Stephen's Green Club in Dublin was running into serious financial difficulty. The Club was one of the few restaurants in Dublin of significant quality and was a meeting place for decision-makers from commerce and government. A number of members discussed the search for a new manager to save the ailing club, and their thoughts turned to the Ennistymon hotelier whom some of them knew. O'Regan was invited to take the job of Club manager. He later confirmed triumphantly: 'I turned the place around and was making a profit in twelve months'.[5]

O'Regan's involvement, and success, with the St Stephen's Green Club gave him further entry to the Dublin network. Two particular patrons of the Club noticed his ability. John Leydon, Secretary of the Department of Industry and Commerce, and Sean Lemass, Minister of Industry and Commerce, were frequent visitors and O'Regan impressed them.

A new opportunity for Brendan O'Regan was soon to arise from these contacts. The flying boat base had been established at Foynes, County Limerick, immediately before the Second World War. It acted as the major refuelling point for air traffic between Britain and North America. As such, it represented a significant window for Ireland into aviation and international commerce. Visiting Foynes in the early 1940s, Eamon de Valera, Taoiseach, was concerned to see the catering facility managed by British Imperial Airways. De Valera was anxious that such a service, with its high international exposure, should be operated by Irish people. This type of national self-respect was seen to be vital to the young Free State, then only twenty years old. De Valera called Lemass, whose Industry and Commerce remit included responsibility for air transport. Lemass and Leydon searched for a reliable caterer: their eyes quickly fell on the Clareman in the St Stephen's Green Club. Thus it was that O'Regan (aged 25) found himself as Foynes Catering Comptroller in 1943.

O'Regan's stay in Foynes was to be short-lived. Following the cessation of hostilities at the end of the Second World War, Shannon Airport opened for growing commercial business and O'Regan's catering operation transferred from Foynes to Shannon. The administrative arrangements for this were centred on a contract with very interesting terms – an example of 1940s style public-private partnership. Under an agreement with the Minister for Industry and Commerce (who was responsible for airports), O'Regan was personally appointed as Comptroller of Sales and Catering (in his capacity as a private independent contractor) to provide a sales and catering service at the airport. The contract provided for remuneration and participation in profits, set out the terms for his use of state property and laid down the requirements of accountability and aspects of procedure for labour employment. The contract granted O'Regan the use of public assets to provide a necessary service to a required standard. To develop the airport business, O'Regan set up his own company, called Sales and Catering Limited, which he owned and controlled. The contract gave him much freedom of action and influence. Jack Lynch, a member of the original SFADCo management team, remarked: 'The agreement made Brendan O'Regan a one-man state company.'[6]

NEW LEGISLATION

In 1947, the Dáil (Irish parliament) approved an act creating a Custom Free Airport at Shannon. The origins of the bill came from an inter-governmental aviation meeting in Canada. The meeting was concerned with the regulation of international aviation. Irish delegates from the Department of Industry and Commerce sought to gain advantage for Ireland from the conference. They brought with them a proposal for designating Shannon as a 'customs free zone' – an Irish contribution to the development of international aviation. The proposal was accepted by the conference.

Opening the Dáil debate[7] to give effect to the proposal, Sean Lemass, Minister for Industry and Commerce, explained that this measure, an Irish invention, would make Shannon the first 'free airport' in the world. The bill provided that goods and passengers in transit through Shannon Airport would not be subject to customs examination. A portion of the terminal building was to be set aside as a customs free area.

In the ensuing discussion, James Dillon, with a retort that was to earn him a place in local folklore, argued that no transatlantic passenger plane would be likely to stop at Rineanna (Shannon) in 10 years' time and that passenger services alone were not adequate to sustain Shannon. If there was nothing but passenger traffic scheduled for Rineanna then: 'we would have nothing in Rineanna but rabbits'. Dillon went on to argue that the only chance of saving Rineanna from becoming 'a rabbit ridden wilderness' would be to make it the most efficient and up-to-date entrepôt merchandise distribution centre in Europe.

Dillon was subsequently castigated by his political opponents for being anti-Shannon, the 'rabbit' reference being used as evidence. But the criticism was misplaced. Dillon did not voice any opposition to investment in Shannon, and the only negative view he expressed represented a healthy scepticism. In fact, his 'entrepôt' comment, that looked to Shannon as a potential hub for international trade, was inherently positive and anticipated the development policy that would be adopted in later years.

The effect of the Customs Free Airport Act was to generate new potential for sales at the airport. O'Regan already had begun selling Irish products to passengers at Shannon and the legislation allowed him to expand his sales by including dutiable items at duty-free prices.

DEVELOPMENTS 1951–56

In 1951, a training school for hotel management was opened at the airport. This was done under the umbrella of the sales and catering organisation. In the same year, the duty-free liquor shop was opened. During the 1950s, shopping facilities were extended to include perfumes and watches. The duty-free ventures were 'firsts' in the history of world aviation; they have since been emulated by international airports throughout the world. Shannon Airport at that time had achieved strong recognition by the airlines for catering excellence. By 1954, the staff in Sales and Catering Ltd numbered 500. A mail order department was opened in 1954.

By all accounts, Shannon was a stimulating place to be in those years. It was exposed to a world of international travel, emerging aviation, new technology and foreign faces. Jack Lynch, one of the Shannon management team, commented:

> The place had a real buzz, and was very exciting. You would be there all night to meet the flights, do your work and then walk around, take the atmosphere. You got to know a lot about the airport and how it worked that way.[8]

By the late 1950s, the Sales and Catering business was substantial – 500 people employed with £1.5m annual turnover. The credibility of the project, and of O'Regan in particular, was high.

The increasing commercial use of jet aircraft created new demands. In 1956, a jet runway was announced for Shannon. This represented a major financial commitment and a considerable vote of confidence by the government. There had been increasing concern for some time at the impact that jet aircraft would have on Shannon. The longer range of these new aircraft would eliminate the need for refuelling and, as a result, declines in air traffic at Shannon were seen to be likely. Shannon had owed its success in the 1940s and 1950s to the fact that transatlantic flights needed to stop at Shannon for refuelling; the emergence of long-haul aircraft removed this necessity. This was a time of impending change. Many commentators reported a palpable atmosphere of expectation at Shannon. Peter Donnelly (one of the SFADCo management team) described this:

> There was tremendous excitement – everybody in the place was talking about development – everybody in the Airport knew everybody else: it wasn't Pan Am with Pan Am, or Aer Lingus with Aer Lingus – everybody wanted development to take place. There was a total appreciation that the place had to develop or else go back to the hares.[9]

In the face of the threat, O'Regan and his group undertook a number of studies into the potential for new business at Shannon – business that would be less reliant on the refuelling stop. In 1955, O'Regan visited the USA to seek sources of new business. He concluded in an internal memo:

We found amongst travel agents an interest in Shannon itself as a free
port transit stop, as well as a definite interest in one, two and three
day tours originating and finishing at Shannon.[10]

From this visit O'Regan concluded that potential lay in mail order business,
wholesale exports and Shannon as a tourism centre. Other possible ventures
included Shannon as a venue for international buyers' fairs. A building was
constructed for this purpose, but never actually used. The visit firmed up
a lot of ideas in O'Regan's mind and a series of proposals were starting to
crystallise.

Behind much of this work lay the enthusiastic support of the Department
of Industry and Commerce. Peter Donnelly remarked:

> The work of the department was very important. They provided and
> managed a well-equipped airport and can take the credit for a lot of
> the development at that time. They made a very active input.[11]

In the mid-1950s, for example, the department circulated a profile of
facilities at Shannon to the American journal *Business International* for
inclusion in a special free ports issue of the magazine. This initiative was
responsible for attracting some significant interest from potential investors.

THE URWICK ORR REPORT

In 1956, the Department of Industry and Commerce engaged the consultants Urwick Orr to study the possibilities for development at Shannon,
both airfreight and industrial/commercial. The suggestion to involve
Urwick Orr had come to the department from O'Regan as Urwick Orr
had previously undertaken work with Sales and Catering Ltd. Through
this work O'Regan and one of the consultants, J. Buist McKenzie,
developed their ideas for industrial development at Shannon. John Leydon,
secretary of the department, reacted positively to O'Regan's suggestion for
an industrial study of Shannon.

The report by Urwick Orr and Partners was issued in May 1957 and it
made a number of recommendations:

1. Air Traffic: The aim was to increase the attractiveness of Shannon to
   transatlantic passengers so as to curtail as far as possible the tendency
   to overfly into and out of Europe. Also necessary would be active

development of the heavy airfreight business and the provision of adequate freight handling facilities.

2. Industry: Promotion of industrial projects as an integral part of air-freight was recommended. Attractions such as freedom from customs formalities and incentives to industry would be critical.

3. Organisation: The report recommended the establishment of a Shannon Development Authority to develop the most effective arrangements for exploiting fully the airport resources.

Significantly, the Urwick Orr team did comment on the integration of the Shannon programme with national development as a whole. The report argued that national programmes were not effective and that the best approach to promote Shannon should be by a local organisation:

> We are convinced that to be effective the mechanism should be set up as far as possible on commercial or private enterprise lines with authority and responsibility to make quick decisions and take commercial risks in a manner that a civil service department is obviously precluded from doing.[12]

Brendan O'Regan commented to the author that this was not a view shared by all the civil servants involved. Some suggested instead that a direct unit of the Department of Industry and Commerce should be sent to Shannon to implement the new developments. But O'Regan thought otherwise, intervening directly with Sean Lemass and persuading him that the civil service structure was not appropriate to Shannon's needs: more flexibility and local autonomy were critical. O'Regan argued that he himself should be given the job of developing Shannon, and that a local company should be instituted to do it. Lemass, evidently impressed with O'Regan's earlier successes, concurred.

In October 1957, Lemass followed through with a memorandum to the government proposing the establishment of a special company for the further development of the commercial and tourist possibilities of Shannon Airport. Significantly, Lemass withdrew the memorandum at the cabinet meeting itself, submitting instead an alternative proposal for the Comptroller for Sales and Catering to be given these wider functions. This proposal was accepted.

Apparently, the idea of establishing a formal company may have been viewed as premature. Lemass later explained to O'Regan that he could not get acceptance for a new state company at this time.

SHANNON FREE AIRPORT DEVELOPMENT AUTHORITY

By November 1957, following the government's decision, the Shannon management team took on the extra tasks. Four main lines of action were agreed:

• Freight development.
• Industrial development.
• Hotel and amenity development to support tourism.
• Advertising and publicity.[13]

The activity had no formal legal existence but nevertheless was given the impressive title of Shannon Free Airport Development Authority by the O'Regan team although, in reality, the 'authority' was a unit of the Sales and Catering organisation with administrative back-up from the parent body.

During 1958 and 1959, work was undertaken along a number of industrial and tourism avenues, with core policies stated to be the pursuit of the development of Shannon as the gateway to Ireland and the establishment of Shannon as an international air junction. The range of effort at that time was very wide, including research, investigating air services, organising the local tourist industry, mapping and surveying potential industrial land. The atmosphere in Shannon in those early days can best be described as a hothouse of innovation, illustrated by Peter Donnelly's comment:

> The talk was all about new freight and new manufacturing interspersed with references to last night's poker or yesterday's golf – we were going like the hammers of hell: you couldn't delegate because there was no one to delegate to.[14]

The personality of O'Regan as a leader, motivator and team builder comes through very strongly in all the anecdotes, highlighted by Jack Lynch of the SFADCo management team:

> O'Regan was a great man to work for, but a terrible man as well. He didn't mind you making mistakes so long as mistakes were not repeated. He didn't want people sitting in offices. He gave you your head.[15]

O'Regan was reported to be good at using people, in the best sense of the word. Peter Donnelly comments:

Brendan O'Regan was super at consulting people, sussing things out, tucking away thoughts. He would take in an idea from somebody, let it grow and develop, talk it through, do it. If it worked, good: if not, learn from the experience. He was going like a steam engine – everybody had to go at the same pace. But he was also a hard man. If you weren't expanding ideas, he would drop you.[16]

Main steps undertaken at this stage included the following:

- Air freight: Airlines and freight firms were contacted. Research was pursued into the potential for both freight generated from Ireland and international transiting freight, and the results were used to lobby airlines.
- Industry: Discussions were undertaken with national bodies i.e. the Department of Industry and Commerce and the Industrial Development Authority. Plans for a number of standard factory bays were commissioned. By this stage, a number of industrial enquiries had been received.
- Passengers: A report was commissioned from Garret Fitzgerald, then an economic analyst with Aer Lingus. The report provided a positive view of Shannon's prospects with Fitzgerald projecting that, even on a conservative basis, total transatlantic traffic should grow from 2 million in 1958 to 3 million by 1965, with Irish terminating traffic increasing from 77,000 to 132,000 over the same period.
- Tourism: A proposal was drafted for the development of nine hotels, and a site bought at Bunratty near Shannon for one of them (subsequently the Shannon Shamrock). These hotels were to be located at vantage points on a projected tour route radiating out of Shannon. Tour programmes were developed jointly with CIE (the Irish public transport authority), involving stops in Ireland for two, four and eleven days. The major objective was to have these included in US wholesale package tours and brochures, and to make US travel agents aware of them. Marketing programmes were devised aimed at US travel agents (such as booklets and information leaflets) and supported by Bord Fáilte, frequently on a cost sharing basis.
- Housing: The 'authority' also reported at this time that it was now apparent that dwelling houses should be provided close to the industrial estate as the nearest large towns were Limerick and Ennis, both 15 miles away. Efforts were announced to attract housing developments by private enterprise.

Significantly, a substantial shift in outlook seems to have taken place over this time. The 'authority' issued two reports, one in 1958 and the second in 1959 – remarkably different documents. The first emphasised airfreight to a dominant extent while other developments in industry and tourism were seen almost as adjuncts to the airfreight business. But by 1959 the second report seemed definitely to be giving airfreight less importance with industrial and tourism development taking on an increasingly higher profile. The reason for this was simple. Payload generation was seen to be the key, and the focus was to be on economic activities that would produce payload at Shannon. At the time, there was comparatively little freight moving into or out of Ireland and most of that was unsuitable for carriage by air – hence the hope to manufacture airfreight.

Peter Donnelly commented that there was a considerable period of hitting and missing at this time:

> But we finally clarified for ourselves that airlines would schedule Shannon only for embarking or disembarking passengers. For a while we had a bit of a fixation for transit traffic that had been the main source of prosperity at Shannon (restaurants and shops) – we had the vain thought that all the airlines could be persuaded to route through Shannon, but we soon caught on.[17]

At the same time, there was a lot of consultation going on – meetings, forming alliances and debates. According to Peter Donnelly:

> Our first approach was to get support from the local people with clout. We brought accountants in, business people, and briefed them. We held public meetings – two of them with 100 people attending each. Everybody thought we were away on a white elephant trail. Many were sceptical. But the public meetings were important. They convinced some people of what we had in mind, and support grew. People began to get very serious about it.[18]

FORMATION OF THE COMPANY

Throughout 1958 and 1959, it became clear to the committee and executives that the informal 'authority' arrangement did not contain enough powers for effective action. For example, as early as July 1958 the Shannon executives reported:

It has been suggested that the Shannon Free Airport Development Authority should be incorporated as a registered company. As at present constituted, the Authority has no legal existence. For the purpose of completing agreements, negotiating loans and generally coordinating business, this position may require review.[19]

Matters moved quickly at this stage so that by December 1958 Lemass had submitted a memorandum to the government proposing to reconstitute this authority into a limited liability company. Lemass had become convinced of at this stage for the need for a separate Shannon company. Once industrial investment enquiries started flowing during 1958, Lemass agreed to establish the new company. The memorandum argued that the Authority needed to have legal status to carry out its functions effectively functions such as contracts, construction, leasing of property and making grants. The central argument of the memorandum was that the most effective way to promote freight traffic at the airport was to establish industries there and this requiried a legal structure.

Significantly, the memorandum did acknowledge the issue of overlapping with other agencies, particularly the national bodies:

> The Minister for Industry and Commerce wishes to explain that the present proposals will not result in overlapping between the functions of the proposed company and the functions of An Foras Tionscal and/or the Industrial Development Authority . . . the Minister is satisfied that industrial development at Shannon Airport will present very special problems with which neither the IDA nor An Foras Tionscal is equipped to deal satisfactorily.[20]

Incorporation of SFADCo

The company was incorporated in January 1959 with the status of a private limited liability company and registered under the Companies Acts. There were two shareholders: the Minister for Transport and Power and the Minister for Finance. The first board was drawn partly from the older 'Consultation Committee' and comprised a mixture of public and private sector, with two local members and six from outside the area.[21] At this stage, there were at least three elements in place that provided a strong driving force. Firstly, relationships between the board and the executives of the company were reported by all participants to be excellent. Collaboration internally was warm and whole hearted with initiatives tending to come from the ground up, i.e. from executive to the board, a practice reinforced by the small size and composition of the board.

Secondly, O'Regan's links with Lemass lent a vital status with the result that support from the department was enthusiastic and reflected a staunch unity of purpose between the civil servants and the O'Regan team. Peter Donnelly remarked:

> The dictum of Lemass was significant in establishing SFADCo: he wanted every civil service department to become an active development agency. He awakened the enthusiasm of the civil servants and they responded.[22]

Thirdly, the legal framework provided considerable freedom of action. SFADCo was established as a limited liability company, with all shareholding by the government. The only purpose of the legislation was to permit the government to finance the new company. SFADCo's legal power came, therefore, from the memorandum and articles of association and were not limited by statute. The memorandum of SFADCo provided wide terms of reference, permitting the company to do almost anything that would contribute to development at Shannon (or indeed anywhere else), listing no fewer than fifty objectives for which SFADCo was established. These included:

- Promoting the business of air transport of every description.
- Developing the use of airports.
- Assisting tourism and transport.
- Carrying out all kinds of commercial undertakings.
- Doing all things to encourage enterprises at Shannon Airport.

In February 1959, Lemass met the board, an important meeting as it demonstrated Lemass's attitude to the new company. Lemass said that Shannon Airport was a national asset that must be exploited to the fullest possible extent. The job of the company was to do this and ensure the continued growth of the airport. There was urgency in this matter. The problem of Shannon Airport's future had become a matter of concern with the contraction of transit traffic. If the problems were tackled with sufficient vigour, additional traffic could be developed and there were substantial possibilities here – tourism, freight transport and industry. Lemass's message had thus two components – the positive exploitation of a national resource, and the counterbalancing of a negative downward trend.

Lemass declined an invitation to sit on the new board, saying that when the necessary legislation had been passed the company would be on its own and he would not interfere with it. Significantly, Lemass actually saw the company as having a temporary job involving a great deal of work in a few years. At the end of that period it should be clear whether the company's efforts were going to succeed or fail. Lemass stated at that meeting:

> In either event it would probably not be necessary to keep the company in existence. For that reason he would prefer that the company should not enter into heavy commitments in regard to permanent staff.[23]

This was to be Lemass's last meeting as Minister with the O'Regan team. He became Taoiseach (prime minister) later that year. The company then came within the responsibility of the Minister for Transport and Power.

Dáil debate, 1959[24]

It was Minister Erskine Childers who introduced the SFADCo bill to the Dáil in October 1959. Childers opened the debate by explaining that the bill provided for exchequer funds to be made available to the new company for factory construction (share capital) and operating expenses (annual grant in aid). He outlined the work of SFADCo in promoting industry and tourism at the airport. He reminded the Dáil that two incentives were already in place – customs freedom for import/export and exemption from corporate taxation for 25 years.

The subsequent debate in the Dáil, and later in the Senate, generated a number of significant policy arguments. These criticisms were important: they set the scene for later debate at administrative level in the years ahead. Three main arguments were raised by deputies against the SFADCo proposal. The most commonly voiced reservation was that development should be concentrated in established centres, such as Limerick and Ennis, as facilities were already available in these towns and artificial attractions at Shannon would not achieve the same success. Because of this, many deputies took the view that development at Shannon should be restricted to purely aviation linked industry. In any event, some felt that the programme was too ambitious, and that the types of industry involved were questionable.

A second view doubted that Shannon needed such a venture. At least one Deputy argued that Shannon Airport could survive without all the

expense of an extra bill, a board, a company and all the extra control by
the State that it would imply. The problem of overlapping was voiced by
many and James Dillon seemed particularly horrified at the thought of
another grant-giving authority. He argued that the proposed grant-giving
power of SFADCo reversed previous government policy to concentrate
grants in An Foras Tionscal (the national industrial authority): 'I am blowed
if I understand that'. Dillon argued that there should be a clear policy:
either one body for all industrial grants, or clearly separate authorities for
different grants, but not a mixture of both as the SFADCo case implied.

Childers responded by saying that the work of SFADCo would go beyond
any kind of development that consisted purely in attracting industry to the
area such as marketing, tourism and airfreight: 'It is a development company in the Shannon area'. Childers said that the national agencies were
not equipped to deal with such a range of different activities and he did
not see the overlapping issue as a problem.

The vision of Erskine Childers

At the same time as the Oireachtas debated SFADCo, Childers wrote a
letter to the new company setting down general policy guidelines about
Shannon Airport developments. Childers wrote that a high proportion of
his observations clarified and reinforced existing policy and that many of
his other proposals were exploratory in character. Nevertheless, the letter
is significant as it illustrates Childers's vibrant enthusiasm for the Shannon
project, and his active involvement in matters of surprising detail. For
example, he suggested son et lumière facilities at Bunratty, medieval
pageants, exhibitions to attract American tourists, a 'what's new' display of
the latest gadgetry and other ideas that even he admitted to be 'of doubtful
practicality'! He proposed a number of new facilities that could be made
available in Shannon and, in cavalier style, declared:

> Let us not be afraid of this proposition. Someone ought to be doing the
> same thing in about fifty places. The lack of such facilities is utterly
> typical of our lack of dynamism. Let us get cracking on enterprises of
> this kind ... the general policy basis ... we assume that the target will
> be reached and we do not look over our shoulders at any moment.[25]

The style of that letter dramatically illustrates the strong political and moral
support that was then driving the fledgling company.

Paul Quigley

The establishment of SFADCo was followed by the appointment of Paul Quigley in 1960 as General Services Manager. A qualified engineer, he brought to the company experience drawn from the Irish Army, manu-facturing industry and the Irish Management Institute. The latter he had built up as its first director. In 1961, Paul Quigley became General Manager of SFADCo.

In the following chapters, we trace the development of SFADCo pro-grammes, and the policies surrounding them – tourism, industry, town development and others. In doing so, we commit the potential mistake of splitting the organisation into artificial categories when in fact these activities were intertwined. Paul Quigley made this point:

> A difficulty in dealing with the history of this company lies in the fact that its tasks, while diverse, were related and even integrated. The approach you take is a logical one but necessarily fails to bring out the extent to which each of the tasks impacted on others. Attention and resources allocated could diminish for one aim simply because another aim had priority at a particular time.[26]

FIVE

Tourism Projects: Castles, Cottages and Tours

THE CASTLES

SFADCo was to achieve considerable notice as a developer of tourism attractions, combining both heritage and entertainment in restored medieval castles at four centres. The extent of these developments was considerable, see Figure 5.

SFADCo's interest in castle development grew out of the decline in air traffic and the realisation that only growth in the numbers of terminal passengers that stayed in the locality would replace the loss in transit business. This inspired a drive for tourist products, attractions, facilities and accommodation in the surrounding area. It was in this setting that an exciting castle proposal emerged.

Bunratty Castle

In 1957 Lord Gort, owner of Bunratty Castle, put forward a scheme for its restoration with the assistance of John Hunt, an archaeological expert and collector of fine art. During the 1950s, Hunt had been undertaking archaeological research at Lough Gur, County Limerick, and had come to live there. Hunt conceived the idea of restoring Bunratty Castle and made some suggestions to Lord Gort. The castle was then owned by the Russell

FIGURE 5

SFADCO CASTLE VISITORS, 1985[1]

Centre	Visitors
Bunratty	262,000
Craggaunowen	48,000
Knappogue	39,000
Dunguaire	23,000

family and Gort's enthusiasm was aroused on a number of grounds. He had been the younger son of a landed English family, amassing considerable personal wealth through prospecting and mining in Canada and becoming a substantial land owner. Gort's interest in restoration arose partly from his own personal connections in the area as his family, the Verekers, had been important landlords in the locality. He had come to Ireland to buy the ancestral home in Gort, Co. Galway but, under John Hunt's influence, he chose Bunratty Castle instead.

The Office of Public Works (OPW), acting then as guardians of the castle (as a national monument), expressed some fears about the restoration proposal. But officials accepted that these fears were groundless. Consequently moneys were invested by both Lord Gort, Bord Fáilte (the Irish Tourist Board) and the OPW in the restoration of Bunratty.

Lord Gort, helped by John Hunt, worked to furnish the castle while restoration was proceeding. To safeguard the interests of all involved, a furniture trust was established to own and protect the exhibits of the castle i.e. furniture and medieval artefacts. Gort furnished the castle with items from his own collection. Membership of the trust was agreed in 1958 to be Lord Gort and Bord Fáilte. The OPW acted as statutory guardian of the castle and did not, therefore, want to get involved in ownership issues. It was also agreed that the operation of the castle was a issue of commercial risk, and not a matter for the trust. The trustees thus decided to ask SFADCo to manage the castle as a tourist attraction.

The OPW was not party to the furniture trust agreement. However, issues concerning the preservation of the national monument in accordance with legislation continued to play a dominant role. For example, OPW officials expressed concern that an entry fee might unduly restrict public access to the castle. On other occasions, OPW found it necessary to control what it saw as unauthorised works in the castle. Some officials in SFADCo argued otherwise. This led to some heated debate between SFADCo and OPW officials although the evidence suggests that these issues were settled amicably. The SFADCo/OPW relationship was seen to be mutually supportive with OPW architect Percy Leclerc taking a lead role.

The castle itself was opened to visitors in 1960. The organisational arrangement comprised the original furniture trust and also a subsequent management agreement between SFADCo and Lord Gort. The management agreement provided a general framework for the development and use of Bunratty. Thus, a partnership approach was now emerging between Lord Gort, OPW, SFADCo and Bord Fáilte. The teamwork inherent in this arrangement was critical. Brendan O'Regan commented:

It would always be a principle that more minds were better than one, getting people together, inviting inputs, skilfully managed co-operation.[2]

O'Regan argued that the initial development of Bunratty provided a good case study of what he called 'managed cooperation' i.e. separate interests working together in a constructive manner, and serving their different objectives at the same time.

A medieval banquet was developed in 1962 as part of a Shannon tour programme. The idea for the banquet originated from many sources and its launch was preceded by a period of intense research and investigation into medieval dishes and drinks, table settings, appropriate dress, programme of entertainment and type of music. The first banquets were experimental with an invited audience. According to Brendan O'Regan: 'We did a once-off banquet for a group of *Time Life* journalists. It worked and took off as an ongoing thing.'[3]

In 1962 plans were prepared for a folk park at Bunratty, beside the castle on land acquired by SFADCo. It was suggested that the castle and folk park should be operated as one unit and Lord Gort readily agreed. The folk park was subsequently developed to include replicas of traditional cottages from several parts of the country, thus recreating the character and atmosphere of post-famine, rural Ireland. A village street was built to provide an insight into small town life in Ireland illustrating the fabric of the late nineteenth century village. In later years, a collection of nineteenth century agricultural implements was donated by Dean Talbot (a local clergyman) to form an important exhibition.

In 1969, Lord Gort proposed to transfer ownership of Bunratty Castle to the State. Concerned that the castle needed to be safeguarded against abuse by any future owner, he felt that the wisest measure was to place it under public ownership. As an interim measure, the castle was given to SFADCo who bought it for a nominal £10,000, the amount being lent indefinitely to SFADCo by the Gort family. However, for some time, there were concerns within SFADCo that the company could find itself in a conflict of interest. One staff member wrote in 1971:

> The castle is not a restaurant. It is a national museum. This is its prime function and source of its importance. When Lord Gort owned Bunratty, he was independent of SFADCo who managed it. There was an authority beyond the day to day management problems and aims.[4]

The view was that the two roles of commercial management and preservation needed to be kept separate with a clear division of functions. This was achieved in later years when the castle was vested in an ownership trust, effectively distancing the long-term preservation of the castle from the short-term concerns of day to day management.

Reading through the files of this period, one is constantly impressed by the unity of purpose shared by Lord Gort and SFADCo. There is no evidence in the files of acrimony or disagreement and a common pursuit was secured. Brendan O'Regan told the author: 'We enjoyed an absolute trust with Lord Gort.'[5] However, this is something that can not be said to the same extent for two other castle ventures, Knappogue and Dunguaire.

Knappogue

Knappogue Castle lies about fifteen miles from Shannon Airport. SFADCo became interested in developing a banqueting venture there similar to Bunratty. At that time, the US Ambassador to Ireland introduced Brendan O'Regan to Mark Andrews, a millionaire from Houston, Texas. The Andrews family were interested in investing in a castle restoration, much of the impetus for this coming from Mrs Andrews, a prominent architect with a strong personal commitment to conservation. O'Regan showed them Knappogue. The Andrews bought Knappogue and, through a legal agreement, granted SFADCo the right to use the castle for tourism purposes. This was through a restoration trust, an ownership trust and a management agreement.

The Knappogue restoration trust was established in 1966, with membership of the trust split 50/50 between the Andrews family and the company. The trust was funded with £50,000, half of which was contributed by the Andrews and the remainder by SFADCo. With these moneys the restoration work on the castle was undertaken. The function of the restoration trust was to restore and improve the castle, using the revenue from banquets and visitors. But ownership of the castle was still vested in the Andrews through the separate ownership trust, although the rules of that trust restricted their right to sale of the property. Thus the existence of two separate trusts was the result of a compromise between two interests – owners and operators. The operation of the castle was regulated by a third measure – a separate management agreement between SFADCo and the Andrews family.

In later years, relations between the Andrews and SFADCo were not entirely even. The arrangements of 1965–66 saw some divergence of opinion, generating arguments about 'capricious' behaviour. In 1976, there was a complaint from the Andrews family about the management of some VIP guests at the castle, and about the handling of publicity for Knappogue. In 1977, the Andrews complained about what they saw as the inadequacy of funds paid by SFADCo into the Knappogue restoration trust. However, Brendan O'Regan told the author that these differences were not of any importance. Knappogue became a locale for a highly successful pageant and banquet, featuring a presentation by one of Ireland's eminent writers, Bryan MacMahon.

Dunguaire

Some stormy relations were also in evidence in a third castle venture, Dunguaire in County Galway.

In 1965, SFADCo leased Dunguaire Castle from its owner, Lady Christobel Ampthill. Unlike Bunratty and Knappogue with their intricate system of trusts and agreements, Dunguaire was an apparently straight-forward lease from Lady Ampthill to the company. Under this lease, Lady Ampthill continued to live in Dunguaire, but granted SFADCo the use of the castle for entertainment programmes. SFADCo was also given an option to buy at some future date. However, the SFADCo solicitor warned at the time that the lease could give rise to misunderstandings but felt this would not be a problem if the parties were amicable.

By all accounts, Lady Christobel was a robust character, with definite opinions of her own. According to Brendan O'Regan: 'She was the very stuff the British Empire was made of.'[6] True to form, by 1968, solicitors' letters were being exchanged between Lady Ampthill and the company regarding who had access to what, who was interfering with who, who could lock the gate, who could do what in the castle, how noisy the banquets were and how late they were held. These differences reflected the inherent tension in the coexistence of a resident owner with a commercial operator. But matters were resolved and Dunguaire today hosts lively banquets for visitors. Lady Ampthill retired to England and sold the castle to SFADCo under the terms of the agreement.

Craggaunowen

A fourth major castle project was initiated by John Hunt at Craggaunowen, Co. Clare. In a memorandum to SFADCo during the late 1960s, Hunt proposed a 'museum complex' for the medieval castle of Craggaunowen.

Hunt argued that the Bunratty project amply illustrated two phases of Irish life – castles of the Tudor period, and vernacular life of the nineteenth century. He proposed a new museum at Craggaunowen to depict the life of Gaelic Ireland that came to an end in the seventeenth century.

In 1969, SFADCo purchased the Craggaunowen site and an establishment council was created to own the development. The idea for this structure was Hunt's, intended to reflect the diverse interests involved. The council had legal existence as a limited company, Craggaunowen Project Ltd., with membership comprising SFADCo, John Hunt, Bord Fáilte and other interested partners. SFADCo managed the property on behalf of the establishment council. Craggaunowen has since developed into a setting for a reconstructed ring fort, a lake dwelling and other presentations of antiquity. The Hunt Collection of medieval artifacts was donated to the council by Mr Hunt. (This was originally housed at the University of Limerick. By the 1990s, a new home had been found for the collection at the Custom House in Limerick). Like Bunratty, the Craggaunowen files are remarkable by their sense of common vision and amicable teamwork.

Relationships between John Hunt and SFADCo seem to have been warm and supportive. About him, O'Regan says: 'We'd be talking all the time, flashing ideas and we'd be in a position to implement them.'[7]

Comment on the castles

A number of conclusions can be drawn from these experiences with the four castle developments, providing pointers for wider developmental issues.

The administration of the castles were meshed in an apparently complex network of ownership trusts, restoration trusts, management agreements, establishment councils and leases. But this range of evidently intricate legal structures had a very simple consequence – to regulate conflict between the partners, to promote cooperation, to avoid conflict of interest and provide for a 'balance of power' between three separate interest groups, each with different goals and objectives.

The use of the castles by the three groups inevitably created the potential for conflict between them and occasional conflicts did surface from time to time. At Knappogue, the Andrews family sometimes took a definite view on what should be done – a view that was different from SFADCo's. At Dunguaire there were some clashes between Lady Ampthill and SFADCo. But none of these differences appear to have been significant. The system of trusts certainly helped here, serving to regulate conflict and cope with any tensions. But within the system of trusts, the

FIGURE 6

INTEREST GROUPS IN THE CASTLE DEVELOPMENTS

Interest Group	Actors	Objectives
Owners	Lord Gort, John Hunt Andrews family, Lady Ampthill	Personal goals (aesthetic, proprietorial, commercial)
Preservationist	Office of Public Works	Preserve national monuments for future generations
Commercial	SFADCo	Visitor attractions

crucial factor was that of the attitudes of the individuals. Paul Quigley remarked: 'All that being said, the big factor was a personality one.'[8]

Peter Donnelly echoed this point about the issue of people:

> In reality, the legal structures were not intricate at all but quite simple. The trusts identified the legal owners and the management agreements were the operating instruments. We seldom ever had to refer to these documents. We just dealt directly with the people involved.[9]

The driving force behind the castle ventures thus emerges as a shared unity of purpose – a common vision and personal agreements between influential individuals, reflecting one of the general themes of the case study: the role of individuals in development, the influence of personalities and the power of alliances and allegiances.

RENT AN IRISH COTTAGE

Growth in tourism during the first half of the 1960s was considerable, increasing concern at both national and local level that accommodation shortages would result.

The idea is generated

This perception about accommodation shortfalls was to generate some very innovative approaches to the problem. In a letter to the Department of Transport and Power in 1965, Brendan O'Regan proposed the establishment of 'cottage courts', groups of five or six tourist cottages with one central cottage to provide reception, entertainment and dining facilities. The cottages would be in traditional style, following the favourable experiences with Bunratty Folk Park. The project would be undertaken directly by SFADCo, in cooperation with other state agencies. The response from Thekla Beere (department secretary) was very positive, saying that the idea appealed to Minister Erskine Childers and further information was requested. But Beere did emphasise that private interests should be involved, such as local hotel groups. In particular she advised that conflict should be avoided with 'entrenched interests'.

The cottage court proposal was further developed during 1966, particularly in relation to private sector finance and management by O'Regan's Sales and Catering operation. However, this latter idea was finally killed off by Erskine Childers who argued in a letter that such direct intervention 'would amount to participation by me in the hotel industry'.[10] But Childers did agree to a minority investment by SFADCo in a private sector company with such an undertaking. Childers's point was that direct involvement would face serious criticism from both the industry and the Department of Finance. By 1967, the cottage court idea had matured into the proposal for Rent an Irish Cottage, a private sector, limited liability company to develop holiday cottages in a number of villages in the region around Shannon Airport. The cottages would be thatched, traditional in appearance, but with contemporary furniture and fittings. The Rent an Irish Cottage Scheme (or RIC as it was called for short) had two related objectives:

1. To meet the growing demand for accommodation around Shannon Airport, particularly in the self-catering or 'rent a villa' sector.
2. To stimulate village development in poorer areas through tourist revenue, improved physical appearance, local employment and local investment – particularly in areas unlikely to benefit from industrial development.

The RIC project aimed to introduce a new marketable element into the national tourist plant, and to provide tourist accommodation that would be uniquely Irish in character. RIC was subsequently formed as a limited company in 1968. The goal was for the public sector agencies to act as animators, or primers, for the initial phase of the project but with an ultimate involvement as minority shareholders. The proposed shareholding was as shown in Figure 7:

FIGURE 7

RENT AN IRISH COTTAGE: PROPOSED SHAREHOLDING, 1968[11]

Organisation	%
Limerick County Council	5
Clare County Council	5
SFADCo	10
Shannonside Regional Tourism Organisation	10
Public Subscription	20
Local Groups	50
Total	100

Keeping the public agency contribution to 30% would secure the character of the new company as private sector and locally driven. The aim was that SFADCo would act as agent for RIC in site purchase, cottage construction, management and marketing.

Finance was to be a combination of:

- Bord Fáilte Grants   33%
- Bank Loans   33%
- Equity   33%

SFADCo would provide certain loan guarantees, and also serve as underwriters for the shares offered to the public. The aim was to keep the board of directors small – at least four and not more than nine.

Initial developments

Sites were purchased first in Ballyvaughan and Corofin, Co. Clare, and meetings were held to attract local shareholders. These meetings stimulated considerable interest but they did raise the thorny issue of local representation: how could local interests be safeguarded? Perhaps each village should have a place on the board, but that would be too unwieldy, while some compromises were discussed e.g. one director per county. Announcing the establishment of RIC, a SFADCo press release stated that:

> The scheme will have substantial economic and social meaning for the villages and may prove to be a breakthrough formula for some of the problems facing the depopulated region of the west.[12]

FIGURE 8
RENT AN IRISH COTTAGE SCHEMES[13]

Centre	Cottages
Broadford	6
Feakle	6
Whitegate	6
Carrigaholt	7
Murroe	7
Kilfinane	9
Holycross	10
Knocklong	10
Ballyvaughan	12
Puchane	12
Corofin	13
Total	98

Market reactions were reported to be very favourable to the initial schemes at Ballyvaughan and Corofin. By April 1969, the SFADCo board noted that the rent-a-cottage idea was a marketing success and to meet the demand it was necessary to provide more cottages quickly. Over the coming two-three years a network of schemes was put in place, as shown in Figure 8 above.

Consumer response was very favourable, with occupancy rates in coastal cottages peaking in summer at over 90%, extremely high by Irish standards. RIC also set the standard for the entire Irish self-catering industry and a number of private sector and community-based projects were modelled on RIC, particularly in Galway and Mayo. The impact on the host villages was considerable, encouraging a number of local improvements following the example of the cottages – upgrading of village environments, shop fronts, hotels, restaurants and amenities. Certainly, RIC was recognised as enhancing the ability of villages to capture tourist revenue. It also provided a morale boost, and a stimulus, in rural areas of low investment.

By 1972, the RIC board felt confident enough to establish its own management unit, independent of SFADCo. The SFADCo board consented.

Growing difficulties

But difficulties were looming. In spite of the initial marketing success, RIC incurred significant losses in the early years. This was explained at the time as the high costs associated with start-up. However, by March 1971, a loss of £13,000 was reported. At the same time, concern was being expressed within SFADCo that many of the company's management services to RIC were not being fully costed and that the legitimacy of this was questionable. There was also concern that the share capital raised from local communities, while considerable, was below target and that the public sector agencies were carrying a disproportionate share of the burden. The shortfall was financed through a bank overdraft secured by SFADCo. Figure 9 shows the shareholding in RIC.

By 1976, concern was continuing to grow about RIC. By that time, the board of RIC numbered no less than twenty-four people, with representation drawn from each village. This was well removed from the small board of between four and nine people originally envisaged, and therefore represented a range of disparate, and potentially conflicting, interests. The scope for unified action was limited here, with endless possibilities for confusion. During 1976 it was agreed within SFADCo to reconstitute and strengthen RIC, and ensure more effective supervision of the running of the cottage company. Later in 1976, the raising of additional share capital was agreed as a measure to tackle the problems besetting RIC. In 1977, the SFADCo board noted that a senior SFADCo executive was appointed to reorganise management working practices in RIC. However, little progress must have been made by these measures as, by 1982, RIC was continuing to report a loss (£19,000), and there was a need for the disposal of assets.

By 1984, further warnings were sounded that an injection of new capital to RIC was needed, and that the quality of the scheme needed to

FIGURE 9

RENT AN IRISH SHAREHOLDING[14]

Sector	Target Shares	Actual Shares, 1972
Villages	97,000	70,000
Agencies	59,000	57,000
Public	40,000	36,000
Total	196,000	163,000

be upgraded. SFADCo felt that it was necessary to strengthen the role of the 'institutional shareholders' on the board of RIC. But the RIC crisis continued and deepened.

By 1985, a loss of £69,000 was reported and criticisms were voiced within SFADCo at management standards in RIC. Privatisation of RIC was seen as a serious option. By the end of 1985, the institutional shareholders were working with some private shareholders, together in a position to hold a majority on the RIC board. Subsequently, after 1985 (and beyond the scope of this study), a number of loss making schemes were sold off. Later, in the 1990s, SFADCo sought to sell RIC to commercial interests and a purchaser was found.

Comment on the RIC scheme

A number of issues with RIC, caused by a series of problems, arose that generated some lessons for wider development issues. Certainly, the product itself was strong and imaginative. There was a growing demand for self-catering accommodation in rural areas, and RIC met this in a novel way. A standard was set for rural tourism. But there were a number of problems which weakened the venture. As Paul Quigley remarked:

> The RIC scheme, in retrospect, was rushed into existence without significant planning. A slower and more patient approach would have been more successful. It illustrates the need for careful planning, structures and measures of performance.[15]

A major weakness was the absence of local control. The villages' only input was shareholding. SFADCo built and managed the cottages directly through the RIC Company. Peter Donnelly observed:

> We were running cottages all over the place from an office in Shannon that was responsible for everything, such as kitchens, utensils, bed linen, painting.[16]

Centralised management caused two related problems. Firstly, it was inefficient and added to costs; all maintenance, for example, was done from Shannon, not locally. Secondly, centralised day to day operations distanced village communities from the RIC scheme and meant that local groups did not have adequate commitment to the schemes. According to Paul Quigley:

We should have left real ownership and management of each local scheme with a local group under some sort of licensing system, with external support of architectural help, standard setting and marketing. Thus each RIC scheme would have been one major element of local cooperation effort. In fact with RIC, local ownership never really happened: that, and local commitment, was the chief lack.[17]

One consequence of overcentralisation in RIC was that quality of the local supervisors tended to be very patchy and uneven. The supervisors were appointed to manage the cottages on a day to day basis. Usually they were local farmers or shopkeepers. According to Peter Donnelly, where local supervision was good, it was excellent; but where it was bad, it was awful: 'You could have a supervisor walk into a cottage with dung all over his boots.'[18]

Apart from the overcentralisation of the RIC Company, other elements were working against the venture. The large board must have been a factor. Such a substantial group of disparate interests could never have shaped an effective team; simply handling the situation would have stretched the most versatile manager, leaving little energy for anything else. Also, the location of some of the RIC schemes seems to have been decided by social, as opposed to commercial, criteria. A number were personally selected by Brendan O'Regan, villages that had a need for development, but with limited tourism potential. Occupancy rates for some inland centres were well below the scenic locations and this drove up costs. A further factor was that the RIC company, while being centralised itself at Shannon away from the villages, was also organisationally distanced from SFADCo, a separation that was hard to manage. Peter Donnelly explained: 'SFADCo never had a solid grip running RIC.'[19]

The RIC experience illustrates the dangers and hazards associated with 'empowerment'. John Friedmann has written how development programmes based on empowerment principles seek to involve groups who were previously excluded from decision-making and argued for 'inclusive development' to allow marginalised groups to reacquire control over their lives and strengthen their capability to define development goals.[20] The significant point is that, in its conception, RIC was certainly founded on those principles and entirely motivated towards empowerment objectives. The fact that these aims were not so easily achieved amply demonstrates the difficulties and pitfalls involved in this approach.

TOUR PROGRAMMES AND PROMOTION

The development of tour programmes, and tourism and air traffic promotion, was a central feature of SFADCo activities from its inception, their prime purpose to increase the flow of airline passengers using Shannon.

Marketing in the 1960s

As early as 1957 an internal note identified four key segments in the US for targeting by promotional activities:

- Airlines executives.
- Charter operations.
- Travel agents.
- Irish-American Societies.

In all cases the objective was to create a high level of awareness of Shannon's attractions using letters, trade advertising, news releases and personal contact. By 1960, a US consultant was being used to do this work. But in 1962 the volume of work justified the opening of a New York office handling two distinct lines of business – press relations and travel sales – with the primary promotional activity being travel trade and media advertising. In 1962, SFADCo launched its first organised tour programme on a pilot basis. This was a 'free day in Ireland' and it gave American tourists twenty-four hours at Shannon, free of charge, including coach tour, accommodation and meals. The objective was to stimulate terminal passenger traffic and duty-free shop sales. The pilot exercise attracted 300 participants and became the basis for a new scheme in 1963 – a 'one day medieval tour' – stopover in Shannon, culminating with a medieval banquet at Bunratty Castle. The outcome was seen to be extremely positive, with 30,000 tour visitors participating by 1966. The medieval tour subsequently developed in cooperation with CIE (the Irish public transport authority) into two, three and four day tours including other areas such as Connemara and Killarney, a first-time venture for Ireland at the time.

During the late 1960s, the medieval tour programme further developed. In 1965, an internal policy document highlighted the following priorities:

- Develop unique qualities of all tours.
- Further enhance medieval tour.

- Develop amenities and physical improvements along route of medieval tour.
- Develop new and complementary tours.

The New York Office continued in its work of public relations and travel promotion. But the high costs of an overseas office for SFADCo attracted substantial concern. As a result, in 1976, the decision was made to eliminate the press activity from the office, and concentrate on travel promotion. A further saving was envisaged by sharing space with Bord Fáilte.

Marketing in the 1970s

During the early 1970s, changes in aviation patterns made the short Shannon stopover less and less attractive to visitors. As a result, the medieval tour was phased out to be replaced by other programmes such as inclusive tours, special interest tours, special activity holidays and incentive holidays. Many of these were promoted on the European market, aimed at tour operator and charter companies. Local organisation and handling was by Castle Tours, a section of Sales and Catering Ltd. It also operated the entertainment at the castles and provided a group handling service for incoming visitors.

But the economic climate was changing. By 1973, poor traffic growth rates were experienced at Shannon. A host of issues was causing contraction: political turmoil in Northern Ireland discouraged tourism throughout the island of Ireland; new fare structures favoured the larger airports with the greatest density of traffic and charter services increased their business at the expense of the scheduled air carriers, further diverting traffic towards the bigger metropolitan airports. The board sought extra financial resources to counter these threats.

During the early 1980s, policy continued to focus on promotional activity aimed at influencing movements of aircraft, passengers and freight. But concern continued to be voiced on a number of issues:

- Air traffic had 'plateaued' at too low a level.
- The airport had financial difficulties.
- There was now a wide spread perception of the airport as an undertaking at risk.

At this time, SFADCo was engaged in cooperative marketing with several airlines then servicing Shannon – Aer Lingus, North West Orient, Transamerica and Air Florida. Owing to the weaknesses of the airport, the bulk of attention was devoted to supporting Aer Lingus. During the early 1980s, the dominant traffic development activity was marketing and promotion, but anxiety was expressed on many occasions that new projects needed to be developed as well. For example, in 1980 there was considerable discussion about the need for creative new facilities to attract tourists. Furthermore, by 1983 there was concern about the need to develop fresh thinking on the concept of creating something big and unique at the airport.

This review of tour products and programmes suggests a number of issues. Perhaps the most important was that the dominant element in the traffic development activity was marketing, as opposed to product development. However, during the 1970s and 1980s a number of concerns were voiced that new products were necessary. Certainly energy was expended but no major strategic breakthrough was achieved − not on the lines of Bunratty in the 1960s. The reasons for this, and the absence of such major new products in the 1980s to match those of the 1960s, deserve discussion.

There are three reasons here. Firstly, maybe the breakthrough of the 1960s represented a window of opportunity created by a unique combination of circumstances, rarely repeated. Perhaps innovations like Bunratty happen once in a generation. Secondly, by the 1970s and 1980s, SFADCo's functions had widened well beyond the concerns of Shannon Airport to embrace a range of regional industrial development. This demanded a substantial slice of scarce resources, with relatively less attention to air traffic development. But there is a third reason. By the 1970s and 1980s the institutional environment was changing dramatically and the unified vision typified by Childers ('the target will be reached and we do not look over our shoulders at any moment'[21]) was giving way to a different type of questioning and policy debate. This type of questioning would no doubt affect the focus of the organisation. We now turn to these institutional developments.

INSTITUTIONAL ARRANGEMENTS

Previous sections have outlined the varied work by SFADCo in the development of air traffic through medieval castles, Rent an Irish Cottage and tour promotion. But these activities were pursued within an institutional environment comprising public bodies such as central government departments and other state agencies, an environment subject to considerable debate and critique, much of which involved substantial argument and internal controversy. The nature of these institutional arguments, and their implications for development, is the issue here.

FIGURE 10

ORGANISATIONAL ARRANGEMENTS AT SHANNON, 1960

Functions	Organisation
Airport management and technical services	Department of Industry and Commerce
Kitchens, restaurants, public shop and duty-free shop	Sales and Catering Ltd
Traffic development	SFADCo

At the time of Brendan O'Regan's appointment as Comptroller of Sales and Catering at Shannon in 1943, the airport was under the direct administration of the Department of Industry and Commerce. By the 1950s, there were two main organisations administering Shannon Airport: the airport management and the Sales and Catering organisation. Operation of Sales and Catering was the subject of a legal agreement between the Minister and Brendan O'Regan personally. The establishment of SFADCo in 1959 added a third organisation to the mix. By the early 1960s there were thus three separate organisational entities at Shannon (see Figure 10 above).

The evidence available suggests that relationships between the three entities were relatively harmonious, and that effective cooperation was being achieved. For example, one document at the time refers to 'success in the development of tourism' being attributable to the 'excellent team spirit' between SFADCo and Sales and Catering. A number of factors contributed to this. The new company in its early years was an offshoot of Sales and Catering and many SFADCo staff came from there. Also, Brendan O'Regan was Chairman of the company and chief officer of Sales and Catering. But SFADCo's relationship to national authorities was a question that was going to be increasingly problematic. For example, an early annual report asked the critical question: why was a local body involved in overseas promotion? The reply was:

> The development of passenger traffic . . . is primarily a problem of attracting more visitors to Ireland and as such it is a national problem, not a local one. The national body responsible for promotion in this field has however made it clear on many occasions that for

success it requires the active participation of local bodies and private businesses who stand to gain from the expansion of the tourist industry. It is doubtful if there is any single organisation in Ireland with so much to gain from international travel as Shannon and it is logical that the company should engage in travel promotion.[22]

This potential conflict between local and national authorities was soon to appear in both relations with Aer Rianta and with central government.

Aer Rianta

In 1966, Aer Rianta, the new Irish Airports Authority, took over the administration of Dublin Airport from the Department of Transport and Power. This obviously raised the issue of Shannon administration. In 1967, SFADCo recommended that the special circumstances at Shannon called for a single body (separate from Aer Rianta) for non-technical services at the airport. A study of the idea was proposed. A period of intense debate and argument followed.

Erskine Childers's immediate reaction was to reject the SFADCo proposal for a single new authority and even the idea of the study. This was followed by an announcement by the minister in May 1968 that Aer Rianta would be given responsibility for the management of Shannon Airport on the same basis as Aer Rianta presently managed Dublin i.e. day to day management. However, he also pointed out that Aer Rianta would cooperate with SFADCo. Apart from straight question and answer correspondence, there is little evidence of any face to face consultation between the minister and SFADCo on this issue.

In August 1968, some months after the Childers announcement, R.C. O'Connor, the new Aer Rianta general manager (previously with the Department of Transport and Power), visited Shannon and met with three officials from the airport management, Sales and Catering and SFADCo. At this meeting, O'Connor was emphatic that Aer Rianta intended to take over all airport functions i.e airport management, sales and catering and SFADCo traffic development activity. This attracted an angry response from O'Regan to the Department of Transport and Power, protesting at the apparent lack of consultation by O'Connor, and arguing against the specific proposals which O'Connor was making. A strong letter was written to the minister against the change, and proposing instead the unification of airport management and development functions in one local agency. A meeting was requested.

But Childers was not to be moved, responding firmly that his decision would not be changed. He said that SFADCo would not be adversely affected, since it never had responsibility for airport operation anyway. In what was to be a less than prophetic statement he wrote: 'it would, however, be defeatist to assume the inability of two state-sponsored bodies to operate in concert'.[23] Childers also rejected the idea of a face-to-face meeting.

This was obviously a difficult period for those involved. On the face of it, the statements by O'Connor that Aer Rianta would take over all aspects of the airport contradicted the Childers view that Aer Rianta should coexist with SFADCo, and that SFADCo would not be adversely affected. At the very least, it was an interpretation that conflicted with SFADCo's. But the critical issue was that Childers's definition of remit was relatively vague and open to different interpretations. The cost of this weakness was soon to appear, for there followed a period of four years of intense debate, discussion and negotiation in which the two agencies sought to clarify their respective roles: who should promote tourism through the airport? who should negotiate with airlines? who was responsible for publicity? who should publish statistics? In fact it was not until 1973 that Paul Quigley was able to report to the Department of Transport and Power: 'I am glad to be able to confirm that the working relationships between SFADCo and Aer Rianta are now excellent.'[24]

From 1973 onwards, the basic relationship was laid down: Aer Rianta took over all aspects of airport operation (including Sales and Catering) but recognised SFADCo as the promotional organisation at Shannon. Any outstanding differences between the two agencies tended to be of an operational nature, worked out within the framework of the agreed arrangements. But significant difficulties did appear from time to time, arising during the 1980s in the case of Castle Tours and in the case of teamwork between the agencies.

In 1980, SFADCo expressed concern at the deteriorating financial performance of Castle Tours, a unit of the previous Sales and Catering (now Aer Rianta), responsible for management of the castle, operation of the banquets and tour handling. SFADCo felt that this entire operation was at risk due to problems in its financial affairs and operating standards. A consultant's report by Stokes Kennedy Crowley (commissioned jointly by SFADCo and Aer Rianta) reported that poor financial results were arising due to high costs. But the consultants also argued that the efficiency of the operation had been seriously impaired by the division of responsibility between Aer Rianta and SFADCo. (Subsequently, after 1985 and beyond the scope of this study, the Castle Tours operation was transferred to SFADCo.)

The second coordination problem arose due to perceived difficulties in ongoing teamwork between the two agencies. In 1981, for example, some SFADCo people were arguing that the centralisation of Aer Rianta decision-making had depressed local initiative and that airport morale was reduced. They also felt that the division of responsibility for airport functions between a number of agencies and bodies militated against action.

So these sets of issues suggest that the interagency agreement of 1973, thrashed out in so much heat, still left considerable scope for argument and dissension. To conclude on the SFADCo/Aer Rianta relationship, the story illustrates some points about organisational interactions from which significant lessons can be learned.

The first lesson came from Childers's statement of 1968: 'It would be defeatist to assume the inability of two state-sponsored bodies to operate in concert.' This is a reasonable comment, but conversely it also assumes that concerted action between state bodies will flow from this. If such was Childers' assumption, then to say that it was unfulfilled is putting it mildly: the assumption that concerted action would flow was erroneous. The basic definition of areas of responsibility were allowed to become blurred. Thus an absence of clarity of roles gave rise to organisational differences with resultant poor teamwork between the agencies.

The second issue is that the idea of a single local agency responsible for both the operation and development of the airport never seems to have been seriously considered by central government, with relatively little evaluation of the idea on the part of the Department of Transport. Perhaps a lot of the subsequent organisational arguments would have been unnecessary if there had been more open debate, consultation and assessment at the very beginning i.e. in 1968. The lesson here is that, before reorganisation, a considerable period of open discussion and critique will make life easier later on for everybody concerned.

But the question can be posed whether the apparent differences between Aer Rianta and SFADCo had any real cost for development, or were they mere 'boardroom battles'. There are contradictory answers to this question. On the one hand, passenger traffic at Shannon reached 1.4 million by the late 1980s, three times the level of the 1950s (see Figure 11). So any organisational differences did not impede this growth, or at least it was achieved in spite of them. Brendan O'Regan commented that many of these conflicts were incidental, no more than normal frictions between government agencies and Peter Donnelly also confirmed that 'although the arguments were long drawn-out, they did not slacken the work'.[25] On the other hand, there is evidence of some cost to the simple management of the inter organisational relationship. It took four years after the minister's 1968 statement to achieve agreement on roles, and even that agreement did not prevent periodic operational difficulties. If there was a cost, then it may have been in terms of poor relationships. This must have had some impact in diverting energies from truly development work or, at the very least, in diluting their strength.

Central government

During the 1960s, there was strong agreement from central government on where the SFADCo priorities lay: 'promoting the welfare of Shannon Airport, with particular emphasis on the encouragement of commercial, industrial and trading enterprises at the airport', according to Erskine Childers.[26]

However, by the 1970s, this consensus on roles was changing, replaced by a different mood that was critical and questioning. In 1973, the Department of Transport and Power was reported to be increasingly ambivalent. While the civil servants acknowledged SFADCo's professionalism, realism and local involvement, criticisms were noted too: central government officials were apparently concerned about the SFADCo tendency to try to divert business to Shannon with 'little regard for the national need'. Crossing of lines with the regional tourism organisation (a subsidiary of Bord Fáilte) and a too-ready approach to foreign air carriers was also criticised. The department's officials also signalled that originally SFADCo was the only body to which the function of Shannon traffic promotion was appropriate, but now there was doubt. The officials argued that the promotion of passenger traffic was in the interest of the country as a whole and should therefore be undertaken by Bord Fáilte, whereas funds allocated to SFADCo seemed to be required in the narrower interest of Shannon. The company's rejoinder was that it was necessary to emphasise the role of Shannon as a growth point to counter the growth of Dublin and to foster decentralisation.

In 1979, the department opposed SFADCo's support for a possible Dan Air licence to operate a Shannon/London service. Later that year, the department again voiced concern over SFADCo activities. Everything possible must be done to preserve the Aer Lingus New York Service, they argued, and SFADCo should engage in no further soliciting of US airlines, as it was then doing. By 1984, the then parent department (Industry, Trade, Commerce and Tourism) was taking an increasingly sceptical view of

SFADCo's promotion of air traffic in New York. Early in that year, the department strongly suggested amalgamation of the SFADCo New York Office with that of Bord Fáilte. Later in 1984, John Bruton, the minister, clearly indicated that a closure of the New York Office was desirable. But SFADCo continued to press the argument that a base in New York was necessary to service its marketing activity.

By 1985, Bruton's questioning had become more critical, sharp and detailed:

- Why was SFADCo uniquely positioned to continue traffic promotion?
- Should the company not discontinue several of its activities, for example selling off package holidays, domestic promotion of banquets, village renewal or Rent an Irish Cottage?

The board's response was to argue that SFADCo's promotion of Shannon Airport arose out of a pressing national need, and that a local agency like SFADCo was best positioned to do it. However, this debate was interrupted by a cabinet reshuffle in Autumn 1985, when Michael Noonan (a Limerick TD) took over the government's tourism portfolio. Noonan held the view that SFADCo was the appropriate agency to promote traffic at Shannon. Matters rested so.

There are a number of conclusions that can be drawn here. Relations with central government seem to have followed two distinct phases. During the 1960s a common view and shared vision seems to have been secured. But this give way to increasing departmental concern in the 1970s and 1980s about overlap and duplication with other agencies. This change in mood was caused by a number of factors. Brendan O'Regan commented:

> Once the original danger to Shannon receded in the 1960s, the frenzy of support died down and the internal cooperation weakened. With the crisis ending, the questioning started.[27]

SFADCo's work in administration had increased with the growth of the various schemes. This involved increasing interaction with the civil service. According to Brendan O'Regan:

> The idea of semi-state bodies with devolved authority is great so long as an organisation works in harmony with the minister and the civil service. But where organisations have to divert energies to defence, there can be difficulties.[28]

The political and organisational culture surrounding SFADCo had changed considerably; the 1970s and 1980s were marked by a different type of thinking in central government. According to Peter Donnelly:

> There were changes of personnel and changes of ministers, and a change of civil service 'culture'. Lemass was no longer there, older civil servants were retiring, new ones coming with development theories of their own, there was a tremendous concern about overlapping.[29]

Writing about organisations in general, Nystrom and Starbuck argue that defining relationships with other agencies, managing functional boundaries and demarcating responsibilities are major organisational imperatives, and must capture considerable energy and attention.[30] In defining relationships with other bodies, a number of choices are open to an organisation, such as:

- Interdependence: The focus in this approach is on collaboration, networking and joint action, with an emphasis on partnership arrangements with other agencies.
- Competition: The other organisation is defined as a competitor: competitive behaviour is adopted in relation to price, quality and range of service.
- Demarcation: The organisation defines a boundary between its functional area and that of other organisations. Energies are devoted to maintaining the definition of that boundary, and justifying its legitimacy.

The experience of SFADCo with institutional arrangements amply demonstrates the complexities involved here. Defining these alternative patterns of interorganisational arrangements calls for substantial energies and skill.

FIGURE 11

SHANNON AIRPORT PASSENGERS[31]

Year	Terminal	Transit	Total
1950	38,200	149,900	188,100
1955	53,000	368,800	421,800
1960	103,400	312,900	416,300
1965	174,400	203,900	378,300
1970	460,000	442,300	902,300
1975	445,400	586,500	1,031,900
1980	560,600	356,800	917,400
1985	662,900	495,400	1,158,300

SIX

Shannon Free Zone

THE INDUSTRIAL free zone at Shannon attracted a large proportion of SFADCo energies and concentration. Its development can be charted through three broad time periods, with different circumstances and policies prevailing in each:

- 1957–68: High growth; concentrated attention on the attractiveness of the airport for manufacturing industry; immense social and cultural changes; highly integrated approach to the development of an industrial complex.
- 1968–80: Growth plateau; fears of labour shortage; integration of Shannon into regional policies; strategy debate.
- 1980 onwards: Renewed interest in Shannon; focus on international services and aerospace sector; concern for technological infrastructure.

In this chapter we will examine policies in each of the three periods, drawing conclusions as we go and ending with some overall evaluations of what happened at the Shannon Free Zone.

THE HIGH GROWTH PHASE (1957–68)

The government decision of October 1957 to grant the Sales and Catering Comptroller wider airport development functions was followed up by immediate action. In November a press release was distributed overseas. The targets were manufacturers or warehouse operations who intended to export and use airfreight. In March 1958, a brochure was prepared that focused on Shannon as a 'Freeport'. According to the brochure:

> For American merchants and manufacturers seeking bases in Europe, the free trade zone at Shannon Free Airport is an ideal location. It is a supple springboard of trade. It helps you jump over the wall of

taxes, regulations, low European costs and other impediments that make it tough to do business in Europe from across the Atlantic.[1]

Significantly, the marketing emphasis in this brochure follows two particular themes with the freedom from regulation taking even greater precedence then the actual financial incentives themselves.

Legislation

At the same time as this initial promotion was taking place, Lemass was laying the legislative basis for the industrial free zone.

The legal origins of the zone at Shannon went back to the 1947 Customs Act which established Shannon as a customs free airport, a freeport where normal import and export laws are suspended thus allowing free passage of goods. The act at the time was aimed at passengers and freight. But it only required some minor modifications to permit industrial development. Lemass achieved this in 1958 through two measures i.e. an amendment to the 1947 Customs Act and a new Finance Act.

Introducing the Customs Free Airport (Amendment) Bill to the Dáil in 1958,[2] Lemass said that the original 1947 Act had aimed to encourage the development of business and entrepôt trade at the airport. This had been accomplished through the establishment of the customs free airport and the elimination of formalities for goods in transit. The new bill, he said, was designed to encourage the location of businesses at Shannon by providing a licensing system of enterprises established at the airport. This complemented the second piece of legislation, the Finance (Miscellaneous Provisions) Bill 1958, providing for tax exemptions of profits of export businesses at Shannon for twenty-five years. Eligible categories included manufacturing, exporting imported goods, repairing and maintaining aircraft and other export air services and trading operations that contributed to the use or development of the airport.

The origin of both bills is interesting. The Customs Free Airport (Amendment) Bill was modelled on customs free zones overseas. In particular, the customs procedures of Colon in Panama were used to provide the basic formula: import, processing and re-export without customs duties or formalities. Other inspirations came from American free trade zones and Hamburg. The Pan American manager in Panama came to Shannon to give advice. The Finance Bill complemented the Customs Bill by adding the tax incentive. Originally, the suggestion from civil servants was for a five to ten year lifespan for the tax incentive, but O'Regan intervened with Lemass and, as a result, the lifespan of the incentive was extended to twenty-five years.

The opposition accepted the two bills as there was no argument in principle but Mr. Sweetman was concerned that some enterprises going to Shannon had no real business to be in the airport at all:

> I cannot see at all why special facilities should be given, merely because an industry plants itself at Shannon, if the industry can function just as adequately in any other part of the country.[3]

Lemass said that he would not disagree with Sweetman's view, but that the industries to be channelled to Shannon were to be those of a special character i.e. industries likely to use air transport.

Early developments

The legislation was just the background for the frenetic activity that was going on. The sense of urgency is typified by O'Regan's comments:

> Things were regarded as impossible by many people. We had to get going quickly. Get some buildings up at all cost. We were in a desperate hurry. We were told that in a year the airlines were likely to remove Shannon from their schedules. We had a major public relations effort to convince the airlines that by leaving Shannon they were leaving a potential market. We had to talk people into believing the vision.[4]

Planning was accelerated by the commissioning of T. Garlands and Partners to prepare industrial site plans and specifications for factory buildings. Marketing at this time included direct mailings to several US chambers of commerce and industries. During 1959, work began on four standard factory units and studies were undertaken of industries most likely to be interested in Shannon, such as air cargo and international financial institutions. Specific countries (e.g. Sweden and Germany) were also investigated.

A number of enquiries were received at this time. Inevitably this range was relatively wide and included some unconventional proposals. Perhaps the most colourful was a project to breed and process chinchillas (small furry rodents) whose pelts were reported to be in large demand, an idea that drew some acid responses. Senator Quinlan had this to say in the Senate in 1959:

Many of us are somewhat uneasy about some of the new industries that are mooted for Shannon . . . this chinchilla industry . . . nothing better than the multiple system of poultry production . . . dubious enterprise.[5]

Fortunately, perhaps for everyone concerned, the chinchilla project did not survive. But it does illustrate that a certain volume of inevitably questionable proposals is a necessary starting point for any industrial base. Two other projects were also developing at this time. W.B. Pink had an investment proposal for manufacturing clothing industry equipment (this lasted fifteen months) and Coamco started to trade in renovated coin-operated slot machines but also closed after a few months. These early investment attempts, although short-term, fulfilled a vital function. Tom Callanan told the author:

None of these survived but they were demonstration projects. We were selling an open field, we were selling a concept. You had something you could show people, investment is about confidence, so we were able to show investors we were serious.[6]

Peter Donnelly confirmed the 'showcase' role of these first ventures: 'The very existence of somebody in a factory created the first surge of serious interest.'[7] However, there are other views about the 'showcase' effect. Paul Quigley reports that he was unconvinced about the value of some of these projects and it was doubtful if these showcases were really helpful. He argued that new locations needed at least one high prestige project, rather than a number of small operations.

The developmental focus at this time was very much on the use of industry to generate air cargo. The 1960 annual report listed ten significant commitments from overseas investors. See Figure 12.

SFADCo reported that three factory bays were occupied, and a further fifteen allocated. The 1960 annual report also highlighted the need for other facilities such as housing, a central canteen, technical training and a boilerhouse. Teamwork with other agencies was very close during this period. For example, there was helpful collaboration between SFADCo and the Industrial Development Authority (IDA), then responsible for the promotion of overseas investment to Ireland. Also, an exhibition of industrial estate products was launched in New York in collaboration with Coras Trachtala, the Irish Export Board.

However, in spite of this outcome, there was some disappointment at the rate of progress. The impact on the airport was not being achieved to

FIGURE 12

OVERSEAS INVESTORS IN SHANNON FREE ZONE, 1960

Company	Product
Rippen	Pianos
Pink	Fabric marking machines
Sony	Radio
Lana Knit	Fabrics
Progress	Floor maintenance
SPS	Precision fasteners
Hohenstein	Plastic buttons
Spee	Wire mesh

the extent desired and the rate of growth of air freight was below the anticipated level.

Factors affecting the location of industry at Shannon during this time were seen to include incentives (factories, tax relief and grants), relatively low labour costs and the availability of air transport. Shannon was marketed by a number of means. According to Brendan O'Regan: 'We used the airfreight concept to promote industry, gave it a gloss, the air-industrial zone caught investors' imagination.'[8] Jack Lynch, one of the SFADCo management team, discussed the approach used:

> Very haphazard, but something happening every day. System of promotion was via the media, not knocking on doors, we got media coverage and people made enquiries.

Peter Donnelly explained it this way:

> We offered land at one shilling an acre with no response. We sent out brochures of an industrial estate with some interest but no takers. We built factories – a manufacturer took one – bingo – the boat was sailing – enquiries, other manufacturers visited, saw men working and were impressed.[9]

By 1961, Childers was ebullient at the Shannon results, telling the Dáil that SFADCo had shown considerable enterprise, vision and flair in attracting industrialists to Shannon.[10] But this view was definitely not shared by the opposition. According to Mr McGilligan: 'The House can accept this without much enthusiasm.'[11]

A number of concerns were put forward in the Dáil debate that all was not so well. How much airfreight tonnage was actually being generated? How many factories were failing? How much native raw materials were being used? How much genuine employment had really been created? One of the more frequent arguments was that industry should have been located instead in established centres adjacent to the airport like Limerick and Ennis, not in Shannon. To this point Childers replied that Shannon was to be an 'air industrial estate'; locating industry using the airport beside the runway would avoid the double handling of goods, and make transhipment easier.

Childers emphasised the point that SFADCo should keep to the principle that Shannon was an air industrial estate and would not compete unfairly with other towns throughout Ireland. But this view of Shannon as an exclusively aviation related centre was to be a source of considerable debate in the years to come.

One interesting indicator of progress at this time was that Shannon was beginning to experience labour shortages in the occupational sector of female operatives. As early in 1961, there was concern at the large number of enquiries from enterprises seeking female workers, reflecting a fear that there would be an imbalance in the workforce between males and females. By 1962, some industrialists doubted the existence of an adequate supply of female labour. There was now a combination of projects, both established and new, putting pressure on the female labour supply. At this time, immediate necessities included improved accommodation at Shannon for females, recruitment programmes and commuting facilities. But the ultimate solution was viewed to be the development of an urban community at Shannon.

By 1963, at least one project had been turned away from Shannon as a result of the female labour scarcity and local employers were being told that SFADCo was now discouraging firms that sought female labour. The policy focus was to be on engineering companies employing males.

But progress was still considerable. By 1962, the first phase industrial estate of 30,000 square metres was fully occupied, and there were plans for expansion of a further 100 acres. Confirming this progress, Erskine Childers reported to the Dáil in that year that the Shannon record was one of considerable achievement.

However, the opposition had other ideas. Their view was that the list of priorities was all wrong, there was high turnover of labour, airfreight impact was disappointing, companies were running into difficulties and there was too much money being poured in: 'as soon as they have made their money, they can fold their tents and disappear overnight'.[12]

The function of the industrial estate continued to be seen as a stimulator of air traffic, but there was now an increasing perception of the significance of industry as a direct employer in its own right. This shift in awareness is illustrated by comparing two annual reports. The 1961 annual report saw the primary purpose of the industrial estate to help the development of Shannon as a cargo-generating airport while the 1964 version emphasised that airfreight potential was by no means the only criterion: capacity of firms to provide employment was also central.

The EI dispute

Industrial relations at Shannon during the first half of the 1960s were relatively good. By 1966, the annual report boasted virtually complete freedom from disputes in the industrial estate. The report commented that only one dispute had occurred since 1960, and that this had been relatively minor. But this good record was just about to be lost.

The EI company was a subsidiary of the US firm General Electric, the largest single project at Shannon, employing 1,000 people, mostly females, in the manufacture of radio components. About 300 of the workforce were unionised but the remainder were not: EI had a policy of never dealing with unions. In 1966, the ITGWU (Irish Transport and General Workers Union) made a claim for improved conditions on behalf of the 300 who were its members. EI refused to negotiate with the union on the grounds that, since the majority had not sought union membership, no union would be recognised by the plant. The ITGWU replied that it was still entitled to represent its own members, irrespective of what other employees wanted.

In October 1967, strike notice was served. There followed a prolonged and bitter dispute, one that called up all the issues of trade unions and multinational branch plants in developing countries. EI claimed that, since the majority were not unionised, no trade dispute existed. It sought confirmation of this from the High Court. The union brought the matter to the Labour Court (an official mediation forum) but EI refused to attend.

The bitterness intensified. There were arguments about intimidation at picket lines, buses transporting workers were burnt and a picket was threatened on the entire industrial estate. Feelings ran high. Jim Tully told the Dáil at that time:

> Never again will a company come in here to try to rub the faces of the workers of this country in the dust as EI are doing at the present time.[13]

SFADCo's approach was to privately urge EI to grant union recognition while simultaneously pleading with the ITGWU not to black the entire industrial estate.

On 9 April 1968, the Chief Justice of the Supreme Court argued that a trade dispute did indeed exist. Two weeks later, on 25 April, the Labour Court recommended that EI recognise the ITGWU as the representative of its members in the plant. The strike ended with union victory, and left no doubt about the legal rights of employees to representation.

The EI strike provided ample lessons for many. For SFADCo, it illustrated the dangers inherent in a single big employer, relatively dominant in one industrial estate (EI accounted for almost one-third of the Shannon industrial labour force). The strike demonstrated what can happen when something goes wrong with such a big operator: large size brings vulnerability with potential spill-overs for the whole industrial estate.

Overview, 1957–68

The Dáil debated SFADCo again in 1968. This time there was fulsome praise for what had been achieved. Minister Childers reported that the company had been making steady progress in attracting new industry to Shannon, and the opposition representatives concurred: 'These people deserve the nation's thanks for the magnificent work they are doing'.[14]

Given the growth record at Shannon, it is easy to see why SFADCo was attracting so much applause.

But after 1968, both the fortunes and policies of Shannon changed. There were two reasons for this. Firstly, in 1968 SFADCo was given an extended remit of regional industrial development and regional considerations came to dominate the agenda for the agency, integrating Shannon more and more into issues of wider significance. Policies towards the zone were to reflect that. Secondly, the international investment climate also changed. Shannon had grown in a period of rapid international expansion in investment:

FIGURE 13

SHANNON FREE ZONE EMPLOYMENT[15]

Year	Employment
1961	463
1964	2,109
1968	3,942

FIGURE 14

FIXED CAPITAL FORMATION IN OECD COUNTRIES[16]

Period	Annual Growth
1960–68	+6.5
1968–73	+5.9
1973–79	+1.0
1979–89	+1.0

Shannon's initial development had coincided with a major investment surge in the developed world and, as the world's first airport free zone, it therefore enjoyed the position of market leader in a growing market – hence the early success. But later periods would see changes in that, the investment climate deteriorating and other competitors entering the market.

The growth period of Shannon in 1957–68 demonstrates a number of themes and characteristics, worth summarising here:

• A highly integrated and coordinated approach to development.
• A lot of learning on-going.
• Rapid social and cultural change at local level.

Coordination

In terms of coordination, the approach taken by SFADCo provides a remarkable case study of so many activities affected by one organisation, illustrated by a number of examples – warehouses, energy, haulage, training, recruitment, industrial relations, public transport, banking and customs.

In 1959, a proposal was agreed by the board that SFADCo should provide a public warehouse and distribution service. Although this idea of a direct service was never implemented, a warehousing complex was developed beside the industrial estate at Knockbeg Point, providing physical capacity for the growing needs of storage and distribution. A boilerhouse was constructed and operated by SFADCo in the early 1960s to generate steam for industry. This was originally powered by turf but later energy was provided by the Electricity Supply Board.

In 1961, Lep Transport sought a licence from the Department of Transport to operate a haulage service at Shannon but this was refused on the grounds that an adequate service was already provided by CIE, the national transport company. In 1963, Cassin Air Transport sought a similar licence and SFADCo argued in favour of both Cassin and Lep providing such services in the zone. The view was that a local freight forwarding sector was a vital ingredient in industrial development. The lobby was successful and the nucleus of a regional freight forwarding industry emerged.

During the early 1960s, direct training programmes were provided by SFADCo for industry, following a report by the European Productivity Agency on organisation for training in 1959. The original idea was that SFADCo would employ industrial engineers and second them to industry to supervise training. The actual training programme provided for operator, apprentice and supervisory training in industry, with one full-time training officer. This function was ultimately transferred to AnCO, the Industrial Training Authority, following its establishment in the late 1960s.

Recruitment programmes were organised directly by SFADCo, focusing particularly on workers in short supply e.g. female and skilled labour. Mechanisms to attract these categories included recruitment campaigns aimed at Irish emigrants in Britain coming home for Christmas. Following the establishment of the National Manpower Service in the 1970s, this function transferred to that agency.

The introduction of new industry on such a relatively large scale and such a rapid pace immediately brought consequences for trade unions and industrial relations. A Dutch advisor (Vermullen) was used to provide guidance on industrial relations issues (the Dutch experience of management/employee relations, involving a considerable number of different unions, was useful). A forum was established at Shannon whereby union representatives met frequently with SFADCo officials. Tom Callanan explained:

> We were introducing investment by companies who did not deal with unions at all. We had to ensure respect for the rights of individuals to join or not join a union, as well as ensuring that we didn't have industrial relations strife.[17]

The impact of new industrial development on the position of the craft unions was particularly sensitive and represented a potential source of considerable friction. As Tom Callanan put it:

> There were rivalries between craft unions, many of whom insisted on being paid a premium for their members. But new technology was making many of these crafts obsolete. There was a new kind of

industrial employee, i.e. machine minders. The structure for industrial relations had to take account of this.[18]

Over a number of meetings with trade union officials, a procedure was hammered out by which grievances could be handled for the whole industrial estate, using two elements. Firstly, the main Irish union, the Irish Transport and General Workers' Union (ITGWU), was nominated and recognised by SFADCo as the primary negotiator for industrial relations at Shannon. Secondly, it was agreed that any disputes between employers and employees would first be mediated by SFADCo before going before the Labour Court, providing an important service to manage and resolve conflict. SFADCo engaged a full-time industrial relations advisor and former trade union official for this purpose.

CIE, the Irish public transport authority, provided bus services to Shannon industrial estate, with ongoing debates about the price of bus fares: fares were subsidised by employers and CIE had a monopoly. SFADCo negotiated for lower bus fares and won CIE agreement to cut prices substantially on the Shannon commuter buses.

Banking arrangements were obviously necessary to service the new industries at Shannon. However, disputes arose between the main banking groups as to who was entitled to claim priority, some claiming that they had monopoly rights. SFADCo mediated an agreement.

Experience with customs and excise systems provides a further vital illustration of the approaches being taken. As Shannon had no port, goods were unloaded at Cork or Dublin and transferred under transit bond to Shannon. The customs authorities agreed to a procedure whereby goods were dispatched direct to Shannon without inspection at the seaports. Customs clearance was at Shannon, an immensely valuable facility in speeding goods to industry. But the initiation of that procedure, and its success, was significantly influenced by individual personalities. The local customs surveyor at Shannon (Seamus Brannog) was heavily committed to the project and senior in the customs hierarchy. He reported directly to the assistant secretary of the Revenue Commissioners with responsibility for customs (Bart Culligan). Significantly the assistant secretary was a personal friend of Brendan O'Regan, a further factor that eased the development of systems and procedures. Tom Callanan explained:

> There was a huge network of influential people working to support the whole Shannon concept: Dr Beddy of the IDA, O'Regan, Lemass, John Leydon (Dept. of Industry), Tod Andrews, Tim O'Driscoll

(Irish Tourist Board) and Jerry Dempsey (Aer Lingus). This provided a huge network where the whole atmosphere was: 'Let's try it'. Of course there were battles over turf and arguments but because the executives down the line knew the bosses wanted solutions, solutions were found.[19]

According to Tom Callanan, the holistic approach was crucial.

We were taking a holistic view of what was going on, and bringing the whole thing together: if somebody needed a work permit, that was done; if goods needed to be brought direct through customs to Shannon, that was done. We were able to look at the total picture.[20]

The evolution of several support services in warehousing, energy, haulage, training, recruitment, industrial relations, public transport, banking and customs is a good illustration of the development of a local industrial 'cluster'. Michael Porter writes that a central ingredient in international competitiveness is the ability of nations and regions to develop growing industrial 'clusters', represented by local growth sectors, together with effective support services in technology, education, research, transport and related sectors.[21] Porter argues that governments should concentrate on a limited number of clusters, and secure effective interaction between industry and support services within each cluster.

Porter shows how such a cluster can give rise to competitive advantage as the geographical concentration of rivals, customers and suppliers promotes efficiency and specialisation, and also innovation and improvement. Rivals located close together will tend to make jealous and emotional competitors. Education and training institutions located near a group of competitors will be most likely to notice the industry, perceive it to be important, and respond accordingly. Suppliers located nearby will be best positioned for regular interchange and cooperation with industry. Sophisticated customers in the same locality offer the best possibilities for transmitting information, making regular exchange about emerging needs and technologies, and demanding quality service and product performance. Geographical concentration of an industry acts as a strong magnet to attract talented people and other factors to it.

The Shannon story is a good case study of the emergence of a local cluster over time, highlighting the difficulties and pitfalls involved in getting support services to grow in tandem with the needs of industry. It also demonstrates the role of local informal networks and personal contacts in the development of clusters.

FIGURE 15

SHANNON TRADE[22]

Trade Type	1964	1966	1969
Shannon exports	£14m	£29m	£38m
Ireland (manufactured exports)	£50m	£97m	£158m
Shannon as % of Ireland	20%	30%	24%

Learning

A second theme, or characteristic, of this period is that there was a lot of learning going on.

The impact of Shannon on the Irish development experience at this time is graphically illustrated by one statistic – export trade. See Figure 15.

The intensity of development in one place reflected a lot of learning and adjustment. Much of this learning was to filter through to the national level.

Within the private sector, there is evidence that technical and management skills learnt in factories at Shannon flowed subsequently to Irish industry. Noel Mulcahy gives a case study of one plant, SPS Technologies, a manufacturer of precision fasteners established at Shannon in 1959. Over the following twenty years a substantial technical labour force was built up by SPS at Shannon, particularly in engineering and precision tool technology. By 1985, Mulcahy was able to identify twenty-eight manufacturing firms, research organisations and other enterprises where ex-SPS employees were at senior management level, a number of them being founders of new ventures. Mulcahy stated that this represented:

> A new armoury of skills to contribute to the development of business and technology in the country . . . knowledge and technology transferred through the activities of the individuals who worked them . . . socio-economic effect of the spin-off expansion of the SPS embryo.[23]

Shannon was the locale for the design of Ireland's first advance factories – standard factory units of about 2,000 square metres built in advance of demand from a specific industrial client. This was a period of much study and research. What size should the factories be? What style of roof? How much office space and provision for storage? Should there be terraced blocks or detached units? These and other questions were answered by experience, with the basic designs used nationally during the 1970s. AnCo, the Industrial Training Authority, opened Ireland's first industrial training centre at Shannon in 1968. Its experiences with this centre informed much of Ireland's training policies during the 1970s. Reflecting this link between SFADCo and AnCo, Paul Quigley became Chairman of AnCo in 1971. Other experiences, such as investment promotion, industrial relations advice and recruitment programmes, were also to provide a learning ground for other agencies e.g. Industrial Development Authority, National Manpower Service and the Irish Productivity Centre.

Peter Donnelly reported that this early period of learning was marked by a climate of innovation and experimentation:

> Initially the SFADCo staff was small in numbers, driven by urgency and enthusiasm. We knew what we had to do but very little about how to do it. Finding out 'how' was a big task. There was no precedent in Ireland, research consisted of:
>
> 1. Consider an idea – if it looks promising, try it
> 2. If it works – fine, modify it, improve it
> 3. If it doesn't – pick up what it teaches and scrap it.
>
> There was no time for formal or sophisticated feasibility studies. It was essential to get industry going.[24]

Tom Callanan echoed this view:

> We tried to use the best of what was happening elsewhere, such as British New Towns, Dutch industrial relations, US technology. We wanted to take best practice from abroad as quickly as we could. We were after all injecting ourselves into a system where best practice was the norm. To succeed we had to be the best.[25]

The role of learning in development, typified at Shannon, has been elaborated by Collingridge who argues for 'trial and error learning' on a step-by-step basis, claiming that decisions must be made by trial and error. There is no way in which choices may be known to be correct and the emphasis must be on experimentation and learning. Collingridge identifies a series of key elements in the trial and error approach.[26]

1. Keep errors to a minor nature: Experiment cannot proceed if the cost of failure is too high and trial and error learning can only occur if the

pain and suffering is relatively modest. Gradualism, and lots of practice, is the critical approach.

2. Change slowly: It is important not to change too much at once because large-scale changes will generate costly errors. Trial and error works with changing things one at a time so there should be a series of marginal adjustments, rather than revolutionary change.

3. Learn quickly: Ensure that lessons are learnt quickly. Learning is impeded if programmes are too long-term. Early completion of a task aids learning.

4. Search for mistakes: Trial and error learning is the search for mistakes so encourage criticism but be selective on what is criticised – focus it on major issues and ignore trivial deviations.

5. Learning is social: Trial and error learning is not solitary – it is essentially social. People, and indeed organisations, working alone can make expensive mistakes. Efficient trial and error calls for many specialist organisations or actors helping to define the mistakes of others. This implies that information must be free to pass between the different actors involved. The participant groups must make rough and ready compromises for short-term implementation, rather than final judgements.

6. Listen to others: A key element in trial and error learning is listening to other people, an aspect with political implications. Listening is a function of the power relation between speaker and audience. If the listener has no power, the voice of dissent is carefully filtered – an exchange of opinion implies a sharing of power.

7. Compromise: Decisions have to be made by compromise between actors with widely differing interests. People thinking alone are notorious for having a distorted view of the uncertainties that they actually face, generating overconfidence. In the case of compromise, the final choice is better adapted to the real risks than the option of any one participant.

8. On-going adjustment: Coordination of decisions by trial and error can be accomplished by the mutual adjustment of many people – no central coordinator is needed. Changes are small which allow plenty of room for people to adjust.

The early developments at Shannon provide a vibrant example of the role of trial and error learning.

Social and cultural change

The third theme, or characteristic, of the Shannon growth period was the dramatic speed of social and cultural change that occurred in one local area.

A report on attitudes in the Shannon hinterland by Dutch researchers in 1960 found significant attitude differences between rural inhabitants working in Shannon, and those still on farms. The Shannon workers sought vocational and technical education for their children, seeing future possibilities for industrial work whereas those still on farms persisted in seeking more high status, white collar work, even though this was less readily available.[27]

Speaking to a conference in the mid-1960s, Paul Quigley reported that people unaccustomed to industry found that changes in their scale of priorities and way of thinking were necessary. For example, haymaking, harvesting and turf-cutting had for generations been regarded by farmers as all-important occupations, but the factory worker is expected to report for work as usual, even during such operations. Furthermore, working indoors for the person accustomed to outdoor work marks a source of further strain. But Paul Quigley also noted that some firms tended to seek the rural rather than the urban worker: 'He is frequently better acquainted with machinery and with the use of tools, and he tends to be responsible and resourceful.'[28]

A study on attitudes to work among Shannon employees by the Tavistock Institute found relatively high levels of job satisfaction, although these seemed to decrease with length of employment.[29]

The foregoing three major themes or characteristics permeated the high growth phase at Shannon, namely a closely integrated approach, lots of learning and significant social changes. A key question here is why was such change achieved with so little conflict and how did growth come so quickly with so little overt social tensions? There were few significant disputes: the EI strike was one and Peter Donnelly suggests that the closure of one enterprise (Sony in the 1960s) was caused in part by a culture clash between Japanese managers and Irish employees.[30] But otherwise there was no significant conflict.

A number of different explanations could be offered: some would suggest a docile rural labour force; others would point to strong national support, but the system of intense local coordination had something to do with it too. The existence of a local programme with a wide ranging scope for action probably helped adaptation and reduced the potential sources of tension. It must certainly have accelerated learning. Hence lessons acquired in any one situation were quickly put to use in others; the adjustment of industry to workers, and workers to industry, was eased and accelerated.

Tom Callanan explained: 'Nothing was simple. The whole thing stemmed from all sorts of networks between people; we were going in so many different directions, it's not possible to follow any single theme.'[31]

THE GROWTH PLATEAU AND STRATEGY DEBATE (1968–80)

The first half of the 1970s was marked by continued plans for the further development of Shannon. In 1972, a decision was made to expand the industrial estate by an additional seventy-six acres and in 1973 Shannon Airport House was converted into accommodation for international office operations. In 1974, development commenced for ancillary small industry at Smithstown beside the industrial estate. Also that year the purchase began of 250 acres for large-scale industry (e.g. chemicals) beside Shannon.

In spite of these plans, employment growth at Shannon slackened from the gains of the early 1960s and remained sluggish for some considerable time.

Some of the reasons for this were contractions in the flow of international investment, compared to the 1960s. SFADCo's first response to this issue was to discuss the possibility of extra resources for Shannon. In 1974, the board noted that it might be that comparatively few extra factories would have to be built in the region by SFADCo, and that funds could be channelled into development at Shannon. The need for diversion of resources to Shannon was mentioned. Within the company, at management level, the same concerns were being voiced. Some argued that Shannon, now with its own resident community, had a need for development as a population centre in its own right, irrespective of the narrower aviation aspects.

FIGURE 16
SHANNON FREE ZONE EMPLOYMENT[32]

Year	Employment
1968	3,942
1972	4,103
1976	3,763
1980	4,454

FIGURE 17

SHANNON FREE ZONE EMPLOYEES: PLACE OF RESIDENCE (%)[33]

Residence	1966	1978
Shannon	18	27
Limerick	38	33
Ennis	7	9
Other	37	31
Total	100	100

However, by 1976, the board was taking an increasingly regional stance, noting that the needs of Shannon Town were not compelling reasons to bring major industry to the area. Such industries should be located where they were most likely to succeed. The needs of other parts of the region should be fully considered, they felt. Many were taking the view that development needs at Shannon were now largely met and that the concentration of effort should be on other parts of the region. In 1978, the board expressed anxiety that growth at Shannon free zone was now proceeding too rapidly, and held the view that employment at Shannon was growing too fast for associated town development to keep up. Continued growth of industry at Shannon could create tensions with other parts of the region, and manpower supply might get overheated. The perceived high level of commuting was viewed with anxiety. Over 70% of Shannon free zone employees commuted from other towns. See Figure 17.

But there were other issues here too. In 1978, there was a considerable realignment of organisational tasks between the Industrial Development Authority (IDA) and SFADCo. Under a government decision, the IDA was given responsibility for medium and large industry outside Shannon, with SFADCo concentrating on small industry and Shannon free zone with a pilot programme for small indigenous industry (see Chapter 9). So the policy debate about Shannon growth vis a vis the region was superimposed on a new division of labour between separate agencies. Also, the new Limerick-based Minister for Industry and Commerce, Des O'Malley, was calling for what he saw to be the need for balance between industrial development at Shannon and the rest of the region.

By 1979 the board concluded that there was a real possibility of full employment in the region. As a result, the excessive dependence of Shannon firms on a commuting workforce could be a threat, both to the firms themselves and to the state's investment in the estate. Thus in 1980, the board made the decision to discourage new development at Shannon apart from aviation related industry, expansion and international services. The key issue was seen to be that, in the long run, the zone should grow in a logical relationship with the town and the airport.

Ironically, this policy debate mirrored almost identically the earlier discussion in the Dáil. As far back as 1961 Erskine Childers had said that Shannon was to concentrate on being an air industrial estate, and should not compete unfairly with other towns.

SHANNON: THE 1980s

Policies in the 1980s focused increasingly on international services and aviation related industry. In 1981, the extension was announced of a special 10% tax rate for new service companies locating in the zone, aimed to help the creation of an aviation related service complex. In 1982, international marketing programmes were launched aimed at service industries in Europe. Over 5,000 square metres of office accommodation was under construction in that year. In 1983 and 1984 internal studies focussed on the need to strengthen the existing base of industry, the impact of changing technology and the infrastructure needed for future investment, particularly in telecommunications.

The 1980s saw a contraction in the first half of the decade, but this was followed by a significant growth in the latter half. See Figure 18.

The policy debates of the late 1970s about constrained growth at Shannon did not surface again in the subsequent decade. There were two reasons for this. Firstly, much of the growth was seen to come from aviation related industry and Shannon was not, therefore, competing with other parts of Ireland. Secondly, unemployment increased sharply throughout Ireland during the early 1980s, pushing any talk about labour scarcity

FIGURE 18

SHANNON FREE ZONE EMPLOYMENT[34]

Year	Employment
1980	4,454
1985	4,261
1990	5,166

FIGURE 19

EMPLOYMENT GROWTH, 1971–86[35]

Shannon Free Zone	+200
Mid West Region (modern sector)	+8,400

well into the background. But the policy debates did put a significant brake on developments at Shannon.

Growth in the modern sector (i.e. chemicals, metal products, machinery and engineering) in the rest of the region far outpaced Shannon during the 1970s and early 1980s, indicating that any policy measures to divert development elsewhere in the area were substantially successful. See Figure 19.

OVERVIEW

One of the major fears in the early Dáil debates was that the proposal to locate industry at Shannon would represent a very expensive white elephant, with high failure rates and an inadequate return for state expenditure. After three decades, it is appropriate to ask whether these fears were fulfilled and whether the Shannon industrial estate generated an economic return. There have been a number of published external assessments of the role of foreign investment in general in Ireland, and also some comments about Shannon in particular.

The industrial policy review evaluated the Irish approach to industrial development, arguing that more incentive was given to foreign firms to invest in Ireland than was necessary.[36] Ireland should respond more selectively by bidding very high on the really attractive projects, and significantly lower on the bulk of potential projects. The policy review made a number of recommendations:

• More focus should be given to projects with a wider range of competitive functions housed in the Irish plant.
• More emphasis on standalone operations without reliance on the parent company.
• More focus on local linkages.

O'Malley commented on Shannon as a case study of a free trade zone. He noted that free trade zones were by no means new, but that the concept pioneered by Shannon was the development of an industrial estate within

FIGURE 20
FREE TRADE ZONES[37]

Zone	Trade surplus as % of exports
Shannon (1981)	59.5
Taiwan (1985)	46.7
Philippines (1973–82)	22.7
Sri Lanka (1979–81)	21.0
Malaysia(1979)	5.3

such a zone with factories and infrastructure provided. O'Malley reported that a major aim of the zones was to boost exports and increase foreign exchange earnings. Estimating the trade surplus, he found a considerable variation between zones in five countries. See Figure 20.

Shannon was found to have the highest level of economic impact when measured in terms of trade surplus. O'Malley concluded that the Irish case showed that the zone strategy can produce some quite positive results in a country with particular attractions for multinationals. But he believed that this alone was insufficient to adequately promote the country's overall economic development.

Data available from the files of SFADCo provide some indications of the measurable costs and benefits of the project. The approach in this case is to firstly define the costs of the developments (measured in terms of grants and infrastructure). This is then compared to the benefits, defined as the proportion of trade surplus that accrues to the Irish economy, thus excluding repatriation of profits from the picture. Costs can be defined in terms of grant payments to industry and SFADCo capital expenditure on land, buildings and infrastructure for Shannon Free Zone. This data is presented in Figure 21.

FIGURE 21
SHANNON FREE ZONE COSTS (£M, CONSTANT 1990 PRICES)[38]

Costs	1960/64	1965/69	1970/74	1975/79	1980/84	1985/89
Capital	31	48	29	22	29	10
Grants	7	13	10	10	27	21
Total	38	61	39	32	56	31

FIGURE 22

SHANNON FREE ZONE TRADE (£M, CONSTANT 1990 PRICES)[39]

Trade	1960/64	1965/69	1970/74	1975/79	1980/84	1985/89
Imports	348	984	747	750	588	563
Exports	426	1480	1340	1508	1447	1525
Net Balance	78	496	593	758	859	962

In the first two decades, the bulk of expenditure was for capital purposes. By the 1980s, grants were increasing as a proportion of total costs. The benefits can be estimated in terms of Irish economy expenditures generated by industry at Shannon, these 'expenditures' defined in terms of the value of direct jobs (measured in wages and salaries) and other indirect impacts (measured by purchases of Irish goods and services). They are suggested by two indicators. Firstly, statistics for merchandise imports and exports from Shannon free zone are available for the full period. This allows us to calculate the net balance of trade, or an estimate of added value. The net balance of trade represents an estimate of the outer limits of the economic benefits of Shannon free zone, the Irish economy expenditures being some proportion of this. But the proportion needs to be defined.

This brings us to the second set of measures. In 1988, for example, net balance of trade was £171m. Of this, about £60m accrued to the Irish economy in the shape of wages and salaries (at £15,000 per employee in the manufacturing sector). In terms of materials and services, the evidence from the Irish economy expenditure survey by the IDA indicates that, in the foreign industry sector of electronics, metal products and machinery manufacture, expenditure in Irish produced goods and services equals that of wages and salaries. Therefore it would seem that, in 1988, an amount of about £120m was injected into the Irish economy by manufacturing industry at Shannon through payments for labour, goods and services, equaling 70% of the net trade balance.

In the past, this ratio would presumably have been smaller: the evidence available suggests that industry increased in its contribution to the economy. Payments into the Irish economy in earlier periods were probably restricted to labour with relatively heavy imports of goods and services. As the quality and range of support services developed, the amount of industry expenditure 'captured' by the domestic economy increased.

In the 1960s, it is likely that about 20% of the Shannon trade balance accrued to the Irish economy, reflecting payments to labour only, a ratio

FIGURE 23

ESTIMATED BENEFITS (£M)

1960/64	1965/69	1970/74	1975/79	1980/84	1985/89
16	149	238	379	515	673

increasing to 70% by the middle 1980s. Therefore a 'benefit' ranging from 20% of the net trade balance in the early 1960s to 70% by the late 1980s, can be said to represent an estimate of the benefits injected by Shannon free zone into the Irish economy. Figure 23 presents these figures.

We are now in a position to estimate the returns to the economy of public expenditure on Shannon free zone. This is done by comparing all the costs (i.e. capital expenditure and grant payments) to the estimate of benefits (i.e. increasing proportion of the trade balance), yielding the following statement. See Figure 24.

The data indicate a number of different trends. The first half of the 1960s was marked by a negative return, with benefits less than cost, representing a period marked by the installation of considerable infrastructure and start-up expenditure. For the rest of the 1960s, and throughout the 1970s, the return to the economy accelerated, rising to almost £12 benefit for every £1 of cost. This return slipped back significantly in the early 1980s as expenditure growth outpaced increases in benefits. However, by the late 1980s, the economic returns had revived considerably and, by that time, each £1 of cost was delivering back £22 of 'benefit' to the economy.

This exercise would seem to illuminate a number of issues.

- Firstly, the initial fears of expensive white elephants were not fulfilled and the data are strongly suggestive of a positive return, with the rate of return to the Irish economy increasing substantially over time.
- Secondly, it shows the long term nature of costs and benefits. Evaluation must be over a considerable time period and any conclusions drawn on the basis of a single five-year period are likely to be inadequate.

FIGURE 24

£BENEFIT PER £COST

1960/64	1965/69	1970/74	1975/79	1980/84	1985/89
£0.4	£2.4	£6.1	£11.8	£9.2	£21.7

- But thirdly, like all statistical statements, it generates still further questions about the extent to which the benefit was dependent on the cost and whether the same outcome could have been achieved with less expenditure. Also, as a rate of return, the question can be asked about how this compares with alternative uses of the same resource and how the net benefit ranks in a comparative sense.

- Furthermore, the costs do not take into account the revenue foregone as a result of the tax incentive. Low rates of corporate taxation are regarded as a cost to the exchequer and a fuller examination would need to account for this.

- While the estimates for Irish economy expenditures are a useful guideline, the data here are national averages – crude and subject to a certain margin of error.

The foregoing considerations thus indicate that the economic benefits of the Shannon free zone were positive and significant, but also suggest that the issue of value for money through industrial development is a relatively complex one.

SEVEN

Shannon Town

INITIAL POLICY DEBATES

THE INITIAL developments at Shannon focused particularly on airfreight, tourism and industry. Housing was not a major issue – the first report of the authority in 1958 made no reference to it. However, by 1959, growing awareness about a potential need for accommodation at Shannon was emerging with the authority's second report noting that, from discussions with groups interested in setting up at Shannon, housing would be needed close to the industrial estate. Plans for a housing estate had been prepared, and efforts were made to have the project undertaken by private enterprise. There had been some discussions on and off about housing and these now came to the fore.

This limited scheme involved a plan for sixty-seven houses, to be constructed by the private sector, with site development finance provided by SFADCo. However, later in 1959, it became obvious that some industrialists were pressing for housing accommodation, but that private sector finance had still not been secured. Consequently, it was agreed that SFADCo should finance a limited number of houses for executive and key workers. In addition, the vision for Shannon housing was unfolding: an area of as much as 500 acres south-east of the industrial area was seen as being a suitable site for future residential development.

SFADCo's first annual report thus announced progress, with a scheme of 137 flats and ten houses under construction by March 1960. During the same year, SFADCo had internal discussions on what the approach to housing ought to be, with the conclusion that housing was central to the success of the industrial estate and that SFADCo should take on the task of building a new town at Shannon. But it was also acknowledged that housing subsidies at Shannon would be no more than anywhere else. This could be a potential source of tension since housing costs at Shannon might be greater than in the adjacent towns of Limerick and Ennis: occupants might thus face higher rents in the new town.

At this early stage, it seems that the issue of housing at Shannon was attracting significant government support. A meeting with Minister

Erskine Childers in 1960 noted the work on accommodation almost as a footnote, without discussion, and, at the same time, the Taoiseach, Sean Lemass, was writing to Brendan O'Regan on how the housing programme at Shannon could be speedily put in action.

The Blaney proposal

At this time a proposal emanated from Neil Blaney, Minister for Local Government. He was then establishing the National Building Agency, a government body to provide housing for industrial workers. Neil Blaney was unhappy to see SFADCo being given responsibility for housing at Shannon and he argued that this should be done by his own National Building Agency instead, pressing Lemass on this issue. Blaney took the view that housing at Shannon was part of the national housing problem, and should be addressed by the national agency that was fully equipped to deal with it. But O'Regan countered this by explaining to Lemass that SFADCo's aim was to develop housing directly, without the intervention of a separate agency. O'Regan's argument was that the housing issue was essentially a local problem, associated with local industrial development and only a local agency with strong ties to the industrial sector would be able to do it. Lemass supported O'Regan on this debate and the Blaney suggestion lapsed. The matter was resolved in favour of SFADCo. But it was not just an administrative argument. There seems to have been substantial personal feelings involved too. Peter Donnelly remarked: 'it was not the most pleasant of interludes'.[1]

Other arguments were beginning to emerge. In June 1960, the Department of Local Government dispatched warning signals about the Shannon housing programme: what was the availability of water and sewerage? was Shannon eligible for Local Government housing loans? where was a comprehensive development plan?

A number of planning exercises were already under way at that time. SFADCo appointed Downes and Meehan together with Frederick Rogerson as town planning consultants. Discussions were put in train with both UK new town authorities and Swedish town planners to exploit the experiences of both.

Growing fears

However, by 1961 there was evidence that the government's ardour for the Shannon housing programme was certainly starting to cool. By April of that year, Brendan O'Regan had to explain to Erskine Childers that the company's long-term programme proposed a community at Shannon for some of the workers only and that substantial numbers would live in other centres too e.g. Limerick. O'Regan conceded that industrial expansion at Shannon would not have been challenged if it could be achieved without the expense of creating a sizeable new community at Shannon. But he argued that the cost of a new community at Shannon would be no greater than that arising from similar employment growth elsewhere.[2]

So Childers must have raised some serious objections to the housing programme. The reasons are not hard to find. The Oireachtas debated SFADCo in July and August 1961, and produced some colourful viewpoints about housing at Shannon. Opening the debate, Childers explained that suitable housing was an integral part of the industrial development at Shannon, pointing out that demand for housing would be related to employment growth and up to one third of the workers would seek accommodation at Shannon.[3] If the deputies' response to the industrial proposals was one of suspicion, then their reaction to the housing programme was marked by downright hostility. Mr Russell (a Limerick TD) argued that it would be more logical to expand an existing community. Mr Sweetman said that it would be far better for adjacent towns to be built up. Mr Norton felt that the idea of living in an airport was abnormal, and other towns should be built up instead. In the Senate, Professor Quinlan was amazed at the grandiose idea of building almost a city at the airport, in spite of the abundance of services at Limerick and Ennis. Senator Tunney saw it as the silliest proposal that had ever been put before a House of Parliament![4]

Interdepartmental committee

With this type of enmity and opposition, it was small wonder that the government proceeded cautiously. At the same time as this Oireachtas debate, the government established an Interdepartmental Committee on Housing at Shannon, comprising civil servants from several departments. They had a brief to make recommendations on the issues of providing houses at Shannon (particularly in relation to the cost comparisons of building at Shannon versus local towns), rents, land requirements, transport subsidies and other aspects.

There were a number of meetings between SFADCo and the committee. But relationships between the two seem to have been uneven, to say the least. By November 1961, Brendan O'Regan signalled to his parent department that an atmosphere of candour was necessary between SFADCo and the committee and that there should not be two opposing points of view.

Later that month, O'Regan disagreed with the contents of minutes of meetings between SFADCo officers and the committee. In February of 1962, Paul Quigley acknowledged that there was a fundamental difference in attitudes between the committee and SFADCo, believing that the committee had an excessively passive attitude towards the need to stimulate development at Shannon, and that its outlook was remote from management and business thinking.[5]

The committee's thinking was certainly remote from the long-term vision then being promulgated from Shannon. In January 1962, a plan commissioned by SFADCo for Shannon was completed. It recommended designating an area for ultimate development of up to 3,000 acres for industry, housing and associated facilities. But the plan also acknowledged that the proposals must be flexible to allow for expansion above, and curtailment below, the size of development envisaged at that stage, suggesting that, with an ultimate working population of 10,000 in the industrial zone, the population could range from 25,000 to 35,000. The plan made general diagrammatic recommendations about industry, roads, central area, housing, social services and landscaping.[6] This was truly a grand vision, capable of sending shudders up many civil service spines. And it certainly did!

In February 1962, the committee issued its report, noting that the SFADCo plans were for 20,000 people over ten to fifteen years. The committee disagreed with this, recommending a cutback to a much smaller community with housing demand to be met outside the airport area. No further land should be bought.[7] SFADCo's attitude to the report was one of rejection, O'Regan arguing that there were a number of recommendations that SFADCo was totally unable to accept, and that these were issues of vital importance to Shannon. While SFADCo considered a possible final town size of 20,000 population, its planning was related to a short-term population target of 6,000 people. This was realistic, he said.

Later in 1962, a further submission from SFADCo argued that the slow development of the community at Shannon was then out of phase with the growth of industry, and that the effect of this gap would be felt for several years to come. The immediate effects were that the company must halt industrial development until the possibility was seen of bringing both sides of the project back into phase.

The issue resolved

In January 1963, Thekla Beere, secretary of the Department of Transport and Power, responded. She said that a government decision had been made on the matter: further housing for workers should be provided at Shannon and that provision for community services should be on a minimum, but expandable, basis. Also, the scale of planning should be related to the smaller community envisaged by the committee, but that this should not be interpreted in too literal a sense.[8] The letter was appropriately vague and open to interpretation. Erskine Childers feared that, if industrial development did not progress as rapidly as hoped, he might be left with empty Shannon houses on his hands. But he seems to have pressed the SFADCo case at cabinet. In a conversation with Brendan O'Regan, he said that Sean Lemass, the Taoiseach, had given him great assistance and support for the Shannon project at the government meeting.

At a meeting with SFADCo officials in February 1963, Childers elaborated on this further. He said that the government had shown every sympathy towards the Shannon project. It felt, however, that it might not be possible to guarantee all the funds for the development of the housing and industrial estate to the full size that the company would like. The company would have to plan the development of the community by stages. The government had gone as far as it could in all the circumstances.

Childers continued to rein in the SFADCo people. Only three months later, he wrote an anxious letter to O'Regan to say that the magnitude of current housing proposals, then being submitted by the company, was well in excess of the scale of planning envisaged by the government. These proposals were to purchase over 500 acres for future housing. O'Regan responded that the then proposals were in the context of a target population of 6,000. O'Regan claimed that SFADCo was making a reasoned effort to forecast what would happen if industrial development continued successfully, and to anticipate the needs of the community as it grew. Childers replied by emphasising that he was keenly interested in the industrial estate and the associated developments, acknowledging that the SFADCo people were living with the problems. But he still said that the then housing proposals were very much in excess of anything contemplated by the government. However, he did agree to 122 houses, site development and piecemeal acquisition of land.

O'Regan replied with disappointment, pressing that the employment prospects fully warranted the case for more housing. At a subsequent meeting in July 1964, Erskine Childers agreed to a scaled down programme of land acquisition of 300 acres.

Childers' enthusiasm for the Shannon project was not in doubt. He energetically discussed at the same meeting the needs of industrial companies: churches, labour conditions, schools, telephone services, gardai and housing.

MAPS

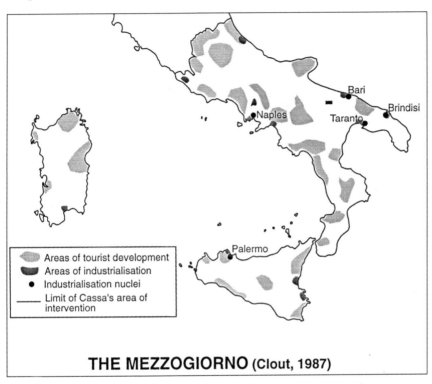

Areas of tourist development
Areas of industrialisation
• **Industrialisation nuclei**
___ **Limit of Cassa's area of intervention**

Bari
Brindisi
Naples
Taranto
Palermo

THE MEZZOGIORNO (Clout, 1987)

HIGHLANDS AND ISLANDS DEVELOPMENT BOARD

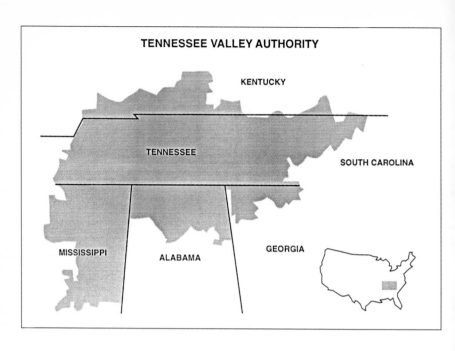

TENNESSEE VALLEY AUTHORITY

KENTUCKY

TENNESSEE

SOUTH CAROLINA

MISSISSIPPI

ALABAMA

GEORGIA

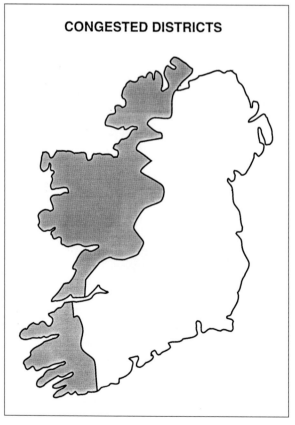

CONGESTED DISTRICTS

Chapter Five

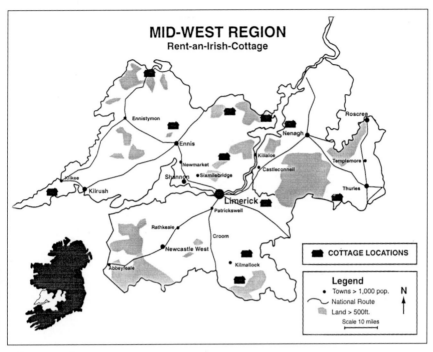

Chapter Eight

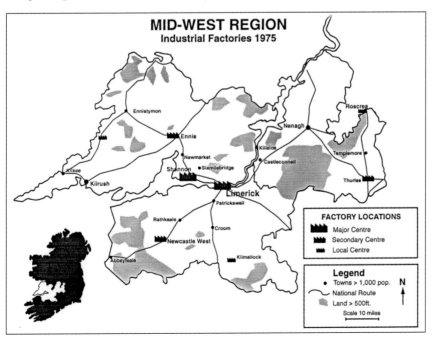

Flying boats on the Shannon Estuary at Foynes, County Limerick in the late 1930's

Next page
Shannon Airport in the 1950's (top)
The site for the town and industrial estate at Shannon in the late 1950's before
development (below)

Industrial development commences at Shannon in the early 1960's

The industrial estate and town of Shannon in the 1970's

Looking at plans for Shannon in the early 1960's.
(L-R) Tom Callanan, Brendan O'Regan, Jack Lynch

Signing an agreement in Bunratty about 1960.
(L-R) John Hunt, Brendan O'Regan, Erskine Childers, Lord Gort

Lord Gort at Bunratty

Bunratty Castle

Next page (top)
Craggaunowen

The Andrews Family at
Knappogue Castle before
restoration

Bunratty Castle singers

Bunratty Folk Park

Lady Christobel Ampthill of Dunguaire

Dunguaire Castle, County Galway

Rent an Irish Cottage

Sean Lemass, Taoiseach, visits
Shannon in the early 1960's

Shannon Town Centre

Raheen Industrial Estate, Limerick

Shannon Airport in the 1980's

Paul Quigley, SFADCo
general manager to 1985

Peter Donnelly, SFADCo company
secretary to 1980

So his concern about housing was to stay within the framework of the government decision, while at the same time promoting the general project.

The discussion about the size of Shannon entered a more positive phase at this stage. In July 1963, the Oireachtas once again debated SFADCo. Childers was on firm ground this time. He explained that housing was being provided in parallel with industrial development, on a minimal but expandable basis. The ensuing debate drew contributions from eight deputies and senators, only one of whom raised any objection about the town proposal. Certainly the virulence that marked the earlier 1961 debate was notably absent: the Shannon project was growing in acceptance.[9] Consequently, the following year, in June 1964, the Department of Transport and Power approved land purchase related to population development of 6,000. A consensus had emerged. But SFADCo still had to tread carefully. Jack Lynch, one of the SFADCo management team, commented: 'We didn't talk about building a town, only houses. We had no commission to build a town.'[10]

The different viewpoints expressed by Erskine Childers and SFADCo provide an interesting example of conflict between approaches to planning. Poulton has shown the difference between various styles of planning, the 'comprehensive' approach focussing on long range goals and visions while, in contrast, the 'incremental' approach aims to make small short-term steps with an emphasis on 'muddling through'.[11]

The discussions between O'Regan and Childers appear to have the qualities of something between a visionary and an incrementalist: O'Regan saw his comprehensive plan for Shannon, embracing industry and housing; Childers and his civil servants saw the pitfalls and the hazards, particularly the political ones. What is important is that the success of the project depended on both perceptions. Without the SFADCo vision, the housing project would never have got going in the first place, but without the brakes applied by Childers and the officials, the project could easily have fallen foul of its more hostile opponents. Perhaps the experience illustrates that such different styles are not really in conflict at all. They are complementary. The trick is to find ways of combining and adapting both to the exigencies of any particular situation. In the case of the Shannon housing project, this seems to have been done successfully.

Paul Quigley emphasised that the two points of view were entirely consistent:

The notion of a 'debate' with points being made coolly and logically from different intellectual standpoints is probably remote from the reality. Childers was a visionary too, but he and O'Regan operated in different realities, Shannon and the Dáil. The view from the coal face was different.[12]

TOWN DEVELOPMENT

The first development of 147 flats began in 1961. Social facilities were also provided by SFADCo, such as a shop, community hall, childrens' play areas and tennis courts, with the hall providing rudimentary school facilities. This initial measure was followed by a housing scheme of 186 houses, and further shops. SFADCo provided sites for two primary schools and a pub and site development for private houses was under way by 1964.

Progress was rapid in the early 1960s, and by 1966 over 400 houses had been completed. Facilities then included a community hall, two primary schools and four shops. Construction of a comprehensive school and a Catholic church was under way. A Protestant church had been available since 1959. With the development of the town, the need became more pressing for a town centre with a variety of shops, restaurants, offices and places of entertainment. Jack Lynch of the SFADCo management team remarked of 1966: 'We didn't even have a pub, so we approached a brewery to develop one.'[13]

Town centre

Scarcity of funds for capital investment was inhibiting development of the town centre. SFADCo believed at the time that if adequate funds were not forthcoming from the exchequer for this purpose, it would have to seek alternative means of financing the project, one possible method being to attract an institutional investor. At this time, tenders were invited and three investment proposals were received. However, by late 1967, SFADCo concluded that all these proposals were inadequate, and would not result in the development that SFADCo sought. It was decided to seek exchequer finance to develop the town centre directly. But, by April 1968, this proposal had been rejected by the Department of Finance. The Finance officials argued that the reasons for such an exchequer investment were not compelling, emphasing that SFADCo would be in a position to control much of the town centre development without actually investing in it. They also argued that if Shannon were to develop into a normal town, sound private investment should be attracted.

As a result, SFADCo went back to the private market and sought further investment proposals. A number were received. In 1969, approval was granted to invite John Sisk, an Irish property development company, to undertake the project. The town centre was finally opened, under Sisk ownership and management, in 1972. But debate about financing and ownership of the town centre did not stop there. At the beginning of 1972, Sisks began to experience difficulties in securing finance for the Shannon town centre project. Consequently it decided to raise the necessary resources through its own property interests. During 1972, SFADCo considered providing direct finance through loans for the town centre, or otherwise buying it outright from Sisk. But, once again, this was rejected by the Department of Finance.

Other developments

Jack Lynch of SFADCo said:

> As the town began to build up, population increased ahead of facilities. There were continuous complaints from local residents: not enough schools, no swimming pool, no cinema, not enough shopping.[14]

In 1967, 28,000 small trees were planted for landscaping because as Paul Quigley said: 'We saw trees as very important for shelter – so important that the planting sometimes preceded final decisions on planning.'[15]

During the second half of the 1960s, other developments proceeded apace. In 1968 a third primary school was under construction. A golf course was opened, promoted by the airport medical officer, Dr Bill Flynn and others. The new town was raised to parish status. A pressing problem at this time was shortage of school places for the young and burgeoning population. Successive annual reports continuously mention this. By 1970, town population was over 3,000 with housing being almost solely provided by SFADCo, as shown in Figure 25:

FIGURE 25

SHANNON HOUSING, 1970[16]

Type	Dwellings
SFADCo	878
Private	65
Total	943

But, by the late 1960s, and early 1970s, concern was being felt at the con-tinued dependence of the town on SFADCo housing and in 1971 the board noted that the policy was to sell as many houses as possible to tenants. Conditions of sale to tenants should therefore be as attractive as possible. By 1972, approval had been secured from the parent department for a tenant purchase scheme, although the scheme was initially restricted by lack of mortgage facilities. SFADCo sought to relieve this by granting mortgages itself. This was successfully implemented. As a result, the tenant purchase scheme grew to the extent that, by 1980, over 1,100 or 55 per cent of houses were in private ownership.

This desire for greater home ownership was complemented by another concern, that of securing a conventional local government structure for Shannon. By 1973, SFADCo was hoping to hand over as many of the town services as possible to Clare County Council. In 1974, national proposals for local government reorganisation[17] suggested an urban district council for Shannon, something welcomed by SFADCo. However, the proposals were never implemented by government.

Concerns about growth

However, later in that same year, more and more anxiety began to be expressed about what was perceived to be the slow rate of town development. In July 1974, constraints on town development were seen in the excessively narrow range of house types, lack of social facilities, high tenancy turnover, lack of private sector mortgage facilities and low levels of finance for maintenance. By October demand for houses was in decline and house building was curtailed. The immediate cause of this was the worsening employment situation, although issues such as the relative attractiveness of the town were also acknowledged to be significant. The 1974 oil crisis was beginning to take effect.

By 1975, policy for town development was coming under further scrutiny. SFADCo recognised that the town had been started to meet the needs of those working at Shannon so that fewer people would have to commute. The need to ensure that the majority of Shannon workers resided in the town was as urgent as ever, but after several years only a small proportion of them lived there. On the face of it, the evidence seemed to suggest that many Shannon workers did not need the town and it was necessary to reexamine why the town was being built. By 1978, the emphasis was on disengagement from company housing, one particular force for this policy coming from the new Limerick based Minister for

Industry and Commerce, Des O'Malley. O'Malley argued against further substantial house building at Shannon. Consequently the board noted that any future role of SFADCo in providing houses would require careful consideration, particularly having regard to the views of the Minister. Later in 1978–80, the debate about town development became intertwined with a related argument about developments on the industrial estate. Decisions were made to curtail industrial developments at Shannon because of the apparently high level of commuting.

The early 1980s were marked by further detchment by SFADCo, continued tenant purchase and restricted house building by the company. By 1984, an internal decision was taken to recommend formal SFADCo disengagement from Shannon town but this was overtaken by a government announcement: SFADCo should transfer its staff and functions related to Shannon town to Clare County Council.[18] In January 1985 a committee was established within SFADCo to organise the transfer. However, later that year, Clare County Council officials argued that their immediate priorities were related to their own financial situation. Evidently, the prospect of transfer was not greeted with much enthusiasm by the council.

There was slow progress. SFADCo acknowledged in its annual report for 1989 that the proposed transfer had still not taken place and that the company would continue to hold responsibility for Shannon town until such time as satisfactory arrangements were in place for the transfer of the town to local authority status.

FIGURE 26

SHANNON TOWN[19]

Dwelling Type	1966	1971	1976	1981	1986
SFADCo					
– rented	453	906	1426	874	818
– sold	–	–	254	806	886
Clare County Council	–	–	20	40	120
Private	12	82	250	409	524
Total	465	988	1,950	2,129	2,348
Population	1,400	3,700	7,600	8,000	8,000

COMMUNITY RELATIONSHIPS

The population profile of Shannon in the 1960s and 1970s was that of relatively young families, heavily dependent on rented housing provided from a single source – SFADCo. Many of the population were skilled, technical or white collar workers – returned emigrants and others from urban areas in Ireland. They were therefore articulate, bringing with them expectations and goals that might not necessarily be fulfilled in the new community. This, no doubt, provided ample scope for tension.

According to comments by the participants, the first years of the Shannon community were typified by a pioneering spirit, informal networks and close personal collaboration between SFADCo and the new residents. However, as the population increased, more formal structures were needed. Thus, by 1964, new arrangements were emerging: the Shannon Community Association was formed to coordinate and sponsor sporting and cultural activities, aiming also to discuss tenancy and common problems with SFADCo on a regular and formal basis. Two years later, SFADCo acknowledged the work of the association in fostering a splendid community spirit. Meetings with the association took place regularly. SFADCo also employed a community officer at this time. Cian O'Carroll (responsible for SFADCo's property administration at the time) told the author:

> Learning from the UK was vital here: the whole role of social workers and community workers; the investment there really paid off. The Churches also had a very big impact – they had facilities and the priests played a critical role.[20]

But problems with community relations grew in tandem with the scale and complexity of the town: so much so that by 1969, SFADCo acknowledged that the problems of communication with residents remained serious. This highlighted the need for a local authority for Shannon. Obviously, the whole issue of institutional structures and local representation was looming larger and larger.

About that time, a social survey of Shannon was undertaken by sociologist Fr Liam Ryan, commissioned by SFADCo. Three hundred interviews were held, representing half the households, and Fr Ryan reported that the general picture of Shannon that emerged was of a community largely satisfied with its conditions. But the people had a high degree of mobility and expectancy, and were impatient with the problems and limitations that life in a new town inevitably brought: 'They have a million complaints, but no single complaint is large enough to unite them.'[21]

In 1970, the Shannon Community Association was restructured to better equip it for the task of representing the residents and in 1971 SFADCo reached agreement with it to establish a planning advisory council. The purpose of this council was to advise on all matters appertaining to town planning. The council comprised both local residents and SFADCo officials. However, if Fr Ryan had noted the absence of a complaint large enough to unite residents, this gap was soon to be filled by a rent strike.

In 1971, rent increases were announced. There followed a rent strike initially by twenty tenants, although this spread to 250 later in the year. SFADCo's approach was to stand firm, and to issue civil proceedings for the recovery of rent arrears. The strike caused the emergence of a new pressure group – the Shannon Tenants Action Group. It was associated with the National Association of Tenants' Organisations, born out of national events: there were several rent strikes in Ireland at this time. Negotiations continued with the new action group and, by June 1972, final settlement was reached. As a result of this settlement, a five year agreement on phased rent increases was drawn up.

The initial announcement of rent increases by SFADCo had been a unilateral one, engendering the hostile reaction. The outcome of the strike encouraged the company to take on a more conciliatory approach to the tenants. For example, around this time, the annual report noted 'increased community participation', and public meetings with residents, and open house meetings between officials and residents. Jack Lynch of SFADCo explained:

> Rents had originally been set in the early 1960s. They were out of date by the late 1960s. So we sent out a circular saying that rents were going up. We didn't consult and there was hell to pay. The result was that various negotiations went on and a phased increase was agreed.[22]

The rent strike engendered further policy changes. According to Jack Lynch: 'It was a watershed. There was much better consultation after that. Other ideas evolved from the same thing – more tenant purchase, home ownership for example.'[23]

In subsequent years, the need for a local authority at Shannon occupied considerable attention and, in 1975, a Shannon Town Alliance Committee was established, encouraged by SFADCo. The alliance brought together representatives from the political parties in Shannon and the Community Association, with its first concern to define a suitable type of local authority for Shannon. This was an important step forward – it assembled, for the first time, the separate political and community groupings. In 1977, a petition was submitted by the committee (supported by SFADCo) to the government for town commission status at Shannon. This represented the most basic authority within the hierarchy of local government. Following considerable lobbying, town commission status was granted in 1981, giving Shannon Town a legal existence. By 1982, the board noted that the recently appointed Shannon Town Commissioners had been very active, but in a 'responsible and positive manner' in matters relating to town development.

SHANNON TOWN OVERVIEW

Town development at Shannon illustrates the point that flexibility in planning is critical, while still working within an agreed overall framework. Certainly the principle, or general policy, of providing for a new community at Shannon has received support. After the debates of 1961–63 there seems to have been little objection in principle. Subsequently, the demand by industry for housing was shown to be significant. Even by the 1990s, there was evidence of considerable interest among new industries in housing for their workers at Shannon. But while the general policy goals had been established, SFADCo officials found that they had to operate in areas of major uncertainty. These uncertainties were almost structural, or permanent, in nature demanding imaginative and flexible responses from the organisation. Four sets of uncertainties in particular absorbed considerable energies – town size, planning policies, public/private split in investment and local government.

On the issue of town size, the medium term target of 6–12,000 population was reached, although the more ambitious forecasts of 20,000–30,000 did not materialise. There were two reasons for this. Firstly, employment growth at Shannon was curtailed as projects were diverted elsewhere during the 1970s in line with regional priorities. Thus the employment base was never big enough to sustain the projected ultimate population. Secondly, the fears of labour shortage arising from a commuting labour force do not seem to have been fulfilled, due to continuing high unemployment in Limerick and Ennis, together with major road improvements which reduced the time and cost of commuting to Shannon. This limited the need for house building at Shannon.

All this generated a gradual policy towards disengagement, privatisation and handover to local government. The issue of public/private investment was one of considerable debate including town centre financing, SFADCo support for other facilities like swimming pools and tenant purchase schemes. There seems to have been no doubt about the desirability of a private sector town but what was debated was the amount of public sector exchequer support for town development.

In the case of local government structures, SFADCo seems to have found itself in an institutional vacuum. Irish local government law makes no provision for new town administration and there are no statutory procedures for handover to a local authority, unlike in Britain where a legal basis is well established for this contingency. So SFADCo had to improvise its own arrangements for interaction with the town community, resulting in a number of novel schemes with varying degrees of success.

Town planning policies at Shannon also changed over the years. The first town plan in the early 1960s was very much influenced by British post-war experiences, but this was considerably modified as time went on. Cian O'Carroll explained:

> The original town plan put a grid on the landscape – straight roads and blocks of housing groups. We evolved later to a different pattern that reflected the features of hills and hedgerows.[24]

If planning can be viewed as the management of uncertainty, then the development of Shannon Town provides on excellent example of this process. The lesson would seem to be that, for uncertainty to be managed, a general policy framework is essential: once that framework is agreed between the parties involved, the surprises and unknowns have a context in which to be handled. Shannon Town is a good example of how such a framework is established.

EIGHT

Regional Industrial Development

D URING 1967, there was considerable debate within SFADCo about possible new directions. In February, the board discussed what the objectives of the company ought to be. They recognised that conditions had changed since the company was established; regionalisation was now under active national consideration and there was a suggestion that the company's resources could be better deployed in the national interest. Options identified at this meeting included concentrating on the development of Shannon, regional industry or regional tourism. The board took the view that focussing on Shannon was still the first priority of the organisation.

This coincided with an emerging national interest in regional aspects of development. National organisations were opening regional offices and the Buchanan Report was about to advocate a policy of regional growth centres.[1] But SFADCo's view that its focus should be on Shannon was soon to be overturned. In October 1967, the Limerick based Minister for Education, Donagh O'Malley TD, announced that the government was considering a proposal to extend the Shannon industrial facilities to Limerick and Ennis and to enable SFADCo to develop industry in the Limerick/ Shannon/Ennis area. This announcement by O'Malley was not un-expected. For some time, the Limerick minister had been lobbying for an intensive development programme for the city. Unemployment was rising, a number of large, locally owned industrial enterprises were closing and the inflow of new industry was limited.

Tom Callanan commented: 'Donagh O'Malley did a sort of UDI on it. He went out on a limb.'[2] SFADCo's response was to accept the new task, while specifying the conditions necessary to make it a success i.e. no dilution of action at Shannon, and adequate power and resources for regional industrial development. But at least one commentator was scathing in his remarks. The *Irish Times* in an editorial entitled *Strokes and Straws* argued that O'Malley's statement made strange reading, and that with 'his penchant for looking after his own' he had engineered a tax concession for

Limerick. The *Irish Times* claimed that this was not in the interests of other areas on the Western seaboard: 'the latest stroke is further evidence of piecemeal planning'.[3] Donagh O'Malley rejected this interpretation later in a local speech in December 1967. He claimed that he was being mis-quoted. He was aiming to apply the expertise of SFADCo to a wider area, complementing any future moves for a University at Limerick, and pro-moting efforts to make the city more attractive to industrialists.

By the subsequent year, 1968, discussions were at an advanced stage on the operational aspects of the new regional programme. In April, George Colley, Minister for Industry and Commerce, met with SFADCo and the Industrial Development Authority (IDA) officials to discuss arrangements. There were different points of view expressed here. IDA officials believed that, in the interests of efficiency, industrial grant-giving functions should remain with them. But O'Regan and Quigley argued that there was a strong case for retaining in its present form the SFADCo machine that had worked so successfully at Shannon. There was a special situation in the Limerick region, they claimed. They were pressing for the status of a separate regional authority with its own distinctive funding and powers.

George Colley expressed concern that pressure for SFADCo-type operations could be sparked off in other regions and he wanted to avoid this. Colley's compromise solution was for SFADCo to operate as local agents of the IDA. However, this meeting seems to have sown seeds of potential conflict between the two agencies: SFADCo was to take charge of building industrial estates and promoting industry, while processing and administration of grants would be carried out by IDA with recommen-dations from SFADCo. Here lay ample scope for convolution!

A month later, in May 1968, the Oireachtas debated SFADCo. Erskine Childers confirmed that it was the government's view that it would be beneficial to make use of the SFADCo experience within the Limerick/ Clare /North Tipperary region. The company would function as an organ of industrial development, responsible to the Minister for Industry and Commerce for that purpose, while reporting to the Minister for Transport and Power for its tourism and aviation functions. This new regional industrial programme was welcomed without opposition in the Dáil; although Garret Fitzgerald did signal a sharp word of warning in the Senate:

> The idea of having a local promotional body concerned with the whole range of local activities operating at local level with local people involved is something that one must welcome and endorse, but the problem of coordinating this local development with the

very split-up responsibilities of government departments is a difficult one. Here difficulties and problems may arise and the answer that has been found so far may not prove satisfactory.[4]

Fitzgerald's comments were prophetic, pinpointing a potential conflict of objectives that was to affect SFADCo for many years ahead – how to achieve the vibrancy and stimulus of integrated local development while simultaneously conforming to the demarcated lines of central government and to national agencies. These were issues that would prove hard to balance.

One such issue was a policy conflict that had been building up since the mid-1960s: the question of the desired scale of development at Shannon, and the extent to which such development should be channelled towards Limerick or Ennis. The Minister for Local Government, Neil Blaney, TD, appointed N. Lichfield and Associates to prepare an outline plan for the Limerick Region in 1967. Tom Callanan said:

> The initiative for the Lichfield study came from Neil Blaney. What size Shannon was a big question then – a big argument around the scale of Shannon. It was commonly believed in SFADCo that Blaney wanted to use Lichfield to control the growth of Shannon.[5]

Other foundations were also being laid for the new developments. During 1968, a proposal to establish a new Limerick Regional Authority was discussed. This emerged out of ongoing liaison between SFADCo and the local authorities. The Lichfield Report recommended that this informal interaction should be constituted into a regional authority, to secure coordination and action in regard to regional planning.[6] The result was the Clare/Limerick/North Tipperary Regional Development Organisation, initially established by SFADCo and the local authorities in 1968.

Paul Quigley defined what the strategies of regional development ought to be. In an internal document written about this time he stated the new priority of SFADCo:

> To ensure the growth of Shannon Airport in trade, passengers and services and to create a healthy prosperity in the Mid West Region through sound industrial development.[7]

Paul Quigley's view was that prosperity should be healthy i.e. avoid many problems associated with development such as prosperity and depression coexisting, industrial strife, cultural diminution and loss of initiative.

Likewise industrial development should be 'sound' i.e. not at excessive cost, or of the wrong type, or in the wrong location, or unrelated to the needs of the region.

WORKING WITH REGIONAL INDUSTRY

Throughout 1968 and 1969, much effort was concentrated on assembling a land bank of industrial sites, and putting in train a substantial programme of factory construction, particularly in Limerick City and Ennis.

Regional industrial programme

In April 1969, a regional industrial programme was prepared to convey SFADCo proposals about the desirable extent and location of industrial development within the region. The study aimed to open the way for consultation and discussion with statutory and voluntary bodies. The programme argued the need to create an 'industrial complex' i.e. transactions between industrial activities. There was a need for some concentration of development to bring about the conditions for self-generating growth, where interaction between industry and services could take place smoothly and readily. This policy implied a main growth centre at Limerick, Shannon and also Ennis with secondary and tertiary centres elsewhere, the programme being strongly influenced by the Buchanan proposals for regional growth centres in Ireland.

Following publication, this document was discussed with local authorities and other agencies and also presented at some public meetings. The evidence available suggests that there were some heated debates, particularly to do with the location of industry and the so-called growth centre policy. Many people seem to have argued that the proposals envisaged an excessive degree of concentration of development in the core of the region.

Tom Callanan said:

At one of our public meetings in Kilmallock to discuss industrial development, we were almost lynched when we told them they were not getting an advance factory![8]

Industrial Development Authority

During 1970, an agency agreement was completed between the Industrial Development Authority (IDA) and SFADCo, aiming to provide operational procedures to facilitate delegation to SFADCo and to maintain consistency in approach between the two organisations. The agency agreement was only forged out of several conflicting points of view. In previous correspondence, Michael Killeen of the IDA had argued that all regions should receive the same treatment in terms of industrial development procedures. Thus the delegation to SFADCo should be equivalent to that of an IDA regional office. But Paul Quigley had claimed otherwise, insisting that SFADCo was an autonomous body reporting to the Minister, not the IDA. Also he did not accept that the approach to industrial development in the Mid West need be the same as that for other regions.

The final agency agreement was an attempted realisation of these viewpoints, although neither side seemed happy. SFADCo perceived that its authority for regional industrial development, as intended by the government, had been abandoned, that the proposed delegation was inadequate and that there were excessive limitations on industrial promotion by SFADCo. But IDA officials argued that they were the national authority for industrial development and had to have appropriate control of funds for which they were accountable. This was hardly an auspicious start to the relationship between the two agencies. Perhaps the Fitzgerald prophecy was ringing true.

But day to day cooperation between the two agencies grew to be very effective. A comment was made sometime later by Paul Quigley that the IDA had a promotional task, and so had SFADCo, with reconciliation coming through common sense and the recognition that each could help the other:

> It can be seen that within a simple 'formal organisation' governing the relationship between the company and the IDA, a highly effective 'informal organisation' has been developed which helps both sides to achieve their purpose. This position was not gained without some friction in the early days but the sparks only lit up the scene and let all concerned see more clearly what they were about.[9]

During 1970 and 1971 other developments proceeded in the region. Provision of industrial estates continued at Limerick and Ennis, as did factory construction at other locations such as Miltown Malbay and Newcastlewest. See Figure 27, page 131. Other support services for industry were also being encouraged: housing needs for industrial workers were assessed with the National Building Agency, industrial relations advice was provided to incoming firms and training courses to upgrade the level of supervisory management were developed with AnCo, the Industrial Training Authority.

Local Authorities

Relations with the local authorities were very cooperative at this time, with common action secured, particularly in relation to the provision of infrastructure, housing for workers and planning. This joint purpose was supported by two factors. Firstly, interpersonal and informal contact between SFADCo and the local authorities appears to have been considerable, providing a basis for a unified organisational endeavour. This informal contact also grew out of shared experiences with the early growth of Shannon Industrial Estate, particularly with Clare County Council and Limerick Corporation. Secondly, the Mid West Regional Development Organisation (RDO) provided an important common forum for debate and exchange of views. The RDO had no executive function, but provided an opportunity for the coordination of agencies, research and information – all at regional level. It acted as a forum for establishing priorities within the region. Subcommittees were established to review progress in a number of areas:

• Education and culture.
• Industrial development.
• Infrastructure.
• Shannon Estuary.

Membership of the RDO comprised Local Authorities, SFADCo and other public bodies such as the Electricity Supply Board, Coras Iompair Eireann and, later, the National Manpower Service.

Differences between SFADCo and the local authorities, where they existed, arose on two fronts. Firstly, industrial location policy generated perennial arguments. Many communities in outlying towns and villages could not accept the growth centre concept for Limerick, Ennis and Shannon and pressed for advance factories in areas such as West Limerick, West Clare and North Tipperary. A second area of conflict was an institutional one, and had to do with the role of the County Development Officers. These were officials of the Department of Finance working closely with local authorities. The role of these officers in relation to manufacturing industry was not fully defined and so generated differences of opinion.

Other developments

In 1973, the Minister for Industry and Commerce, Justin Keating, visited Shannon. Keating's views were very supportive of what SFADCo was doing. He focussed particularly on the development prospects of the Shannon Estuary, regionalisation and the potential for state equity participation in private sector companies. Also, during 1973, the shape and pattern of industrial development was beginning to emerge. Particular topics of debate within SFADCo at this time included a number of issues, such as:

• Poor development in some centres, such as Thurles.
• Difficulties with industrial relations in Limerick, particularly in large firms.
• The Shannon Estuary as a location for industry.
• The need for a wider distribution of new jobs.

Other innovations at this time included the establishment of the Rural Housing Organisation by Fr Harry Bohan, a social affairs consultant with SFADCo. This was a voluntary organisation with which several SFADCo staff were individually associated. The board discussed how this group could be helped by the company.

In 1974, the Oireachtas once again debated SFADCo. Introducing the SFADCo Bill in the Dail, Justin Keating very forcefully took the view that the agency had a broad based regional development goal:

> The company's present aim can be summarised as being the economic development of the entire region for which the continued development of Shannon is an essential feature.[10]

The subsequent debate was thoroughly supportive of the agency with particular comments about dynamism, innovation, breakthrough, imagination, a model region, comments that echoed the strong public confidence in development programmes during the early 1970s. Criticisms, both in the Dáil and Senate, tended to focus on three issues: possible overreliance on foreign industry, poor development in peripheral rural areas and problems with community spirit in Shannon Town.

Within SFADCo during 1974, a number of issues were generating concern. Scarcity of skilled labour was attracting increasing attention and there were continued fears about bad industrial relations. These problems were seen to be especially acute in some relatively large enterprises like the Ferenka steelchord plant (1,400 employed). Infrastructural shortages in Limerick City represented a third factor seen to constrain regional growth.

Activities pursued round this time included a number of measures to support regional industry:

- An industrial liaison service coordinated different public services to industry, particularly in relation to materials and subsupply.
- An industrial relations advisory service provided advice on industrial relations to incoming industry.
- Several studies were undertaken to investigate the economic potential of the region: maritime industrial development on the Shannon Estuary and community resources in County Clare being among them.
- Training programmes for supervisors were expanded and developed and, by 1975, over 100 supervisors were attending these courses annually.
- As a result of this experience, a proposal emerged to establish a Regional Management Centre. This was a combined proposal between three agencies – SFADCo, AnCo and the National Institute for Higher Education (today the University of Limerick), arising out of a working group study by staff from the three agencies. The objective of the centre was to provide functional management training courses on a self-financing basis, with staff initially seconded from SFADCo. By the late 1980s this had developed into the Plassey Management and Technology Centre, a self-financing private operation providing for over 1,000 part-time students per year through open management programmes, day courses and other activities.

The Regional Management Centre was one venture that emerged out of the interactions between the then National Institute for Higher Education and SFADCo.

University of Limerick

The origins of the University of Limerick appeared in the early 1960s with a local campaign for a university. Lichfield supported this through a supplementary study on higher education in the region. The local campaign was complemented by several other trends: concern was growing for indigenous skills in management and technology; the OECD Report *Investment in Education* had just been published; proposals were afloat for a network of regional technical colleges in Ireland and free post-primary education was being introduced. The first official support came from a statement by Brian Lenihan, Minister for Education in 1969. This was an announcement for a new institution with a vision different from that of other Irish universities and more similar to the Technological Universities of North America and The Netherlands.

Opposition to the proposal came from a number of quarters. At national level, there were some major qualms about the idea, with resistance from the established universities. Even locally a number of concerns were voiced. Tom Callanan said:

> Many people saw the new institute as a technical college – they wanted a traditional college with law, medicine and so on. But we had to link with the university movement locally. We had to give it a technological bias to reflect the real and urgent needs of the time.[11]

A planning board was established, chaired by the newly appointed director, Dr. Edward Walsh. This provided a basic planning framework for the new NIHE with seven members including Paul Quigley of SFADCo. A site was chosen at Plassey, Castletroy, Limerick on land which was owned by SFADCo (previously purchased for an industrial project that failed to materialise). SFADCo transferred the land to the new institute. Choice of the site was made following an investigation by the RDO. Paul Quigley became chairman of the governing body of the NIHE. The campus was opened in 1972 with programmes in business, engineering, humanities and science. The NIHE at that time incorporated a number of academic innovations for Ireland – modular credit structure, continuous assessment and cooperative education. The theme of NIHE aimed to be technological, with a strong content of humanities and a substantial European orientation.

The involvement of the SFADCo chief executive in the governing body of a future university was seen to encourage it to relate to economic development in terms of relevance of the curriculum to the needs of the workplace, promotion of contract research by academics, development of a technological park at Plassey and stimulation of joint SFADCo/NIHE initiatives in training, microelectronics and other areas. In a 1973 paper, Paul Quigley highlighted what he saw as incidental benefits of university education in regional economic development:

- Provides skilled manpower.
- Enable graduates to acquire relevant knowledge.
- Creates resources for research and development.
- Improves the living environment for industrial staff and their families.
- Generates direct economic activity in its own right.[12]

This perception of interaction between the university and the region significantly influenced SFADCo's approach to the new NIHE.

Meanwhile, SFADCo's concerns for regional industry were dominated by the worsening economic situation. By the end of 1975, the growth of previous years had been transformed into severe contraction and job losses, a consequence of the first oil crisis in 1974. Necessary actions were seen to be:

- Early detection of threatened firms.
- Eliminating obstacles that inhibit development of industry.
- Fostering small industry.
- Identifying firms with expansion potential.
- Promoting the service sector.

But by 1977, these policy discussions at board level had taken a new direction, one that was to lead to a dramatic shift in SFADCo's approach to development. What these discussions were, and the new lead they generated, is the subject of chapter 9.

REGIONAL INDUSTRIAL DEVELOPMENT: CONTRASTING VERDICTS

1977 was thus the last year of the SFADCo regional programme in its shape at that time. The programme had several consequences for the region. There were, however, different perspectives on, and judgements of, these results, contradictory to each other, as exemplified by comments from Justin Keating and Des O'Malley. In March 1977, Justin Keating paid what was to be his last visit to Shannon as SFADCo's Minister. In a meeting with SFADCo management, he pointed to a number of issues, highlighting the development of basic regional infrastructure and SFADCo's role in this.

> And you've been building, and building, and building with great success infrastructure of all kinds, whether that means water mains or whether it means an Institute for Higher Education.[13]

Keating's second point was that economic geography had a major part to play in any perspective on Irish development. He argued that countries dominated by any one city are damned in terms of their planning with the big city sucking in the rest of the country. Justin Keating claimed that in the sensible economic geography for Ireland, there needed to be countervailing forces of roughly similar size – each big enough to support culture and third level education, with efficient transportation and communications.

This is the sort of economic geography that will guarantee us growth but it would guarantee us a civilised environment as well. And I think you should be planning to be a countervailing force on that scale. I think your fundamentals are that good that you can think in that perspective.[14]

Keating's vision was that of broad based, regional economic development, generating a local climate for growth as an alternative to the Dublin metropolis, a view closely conforming to what he saw SFADCo doing. But Keating's visit was shortly followed by a general election and change of government with a new industry minister – Des O'Malley, a Limerick based TD.

Soon after, O'Malley visited Shannon in his new role as Minister for Industry and Commerce. His comments were sharply critical, and considerably different to Keating's, reflecting contrasts between the two men: O'Malley with a local perspective and Keating with a more national viewpoint, echoing perhaps also differences in development outlook and philosophy. O'Malley said that he had the impression that SFADCo had a fence around it at Shannon Airport, was concerned largely with the development of Shannon and had little interest in the region. He criticised what appeared to be an effort to build a town from nothing when towns around it were dying. He felt that the time had come for fundamental rethinking in connection with SFADCo's role in industrial development. Ireland needed to move away from the reliance on inward investment that had been a major part of industrial policy, but the country could not yet enjoy the luxury of doing that because of the employment situation. Perhaps, O'Malley suggested, over the next two to three years, SFADCo could get the ground work done in relation to the encouragement of local enterprise.[15]

O'Malley's criticisms were not necessarily negative. Paul Quigley remarked: 'Once he got it off his chest, the criticism did not affect his attitude. Des O'Malley was supportive.'[16] Des O'Malley later clarified what he meant at the time:

SFADCo was supposed to be a regional organisation but perceptions in Limerick and Ennis were that it was predominantly airport-related. Although the agency had the powers, actual activities outside Shannon were very limited.[17]

O'Malley explained that SFADCo's original role had been to develop the airport and, because of this fact, it had come to be dominated by airport type activities. The airport had survived so SFADCo should be branching out: 'The key point was that the whole region should grow industrially, not just at Shannon.'[18]

O'Malley told SFADCo that all this was an open question, and that he knew that the SFADCo board were thinking about this anyway. The board had, in fact, been having considerable debate about SFADCo priorities and a debate had been under way for some years. It was into this debate that O'Malley had entered. We will now turn to the nature of these discussions, and their consequences.

FIGURE 27

SFADCO FACTORIES, 1975[19]

Location	Units	Square Feet
Limerick City	17	318,000
Limerick County		
Newcastlewest	3	84,500
Kilmallock	1	13,700
Knocklong	1	7,000
Clare		
Ennis	2	37,500
Miltown Malbay	1	7,000
Shannon	149	1,924,800
Tipperary (NR)		
Thurles	4	65,100
Roscrea	1	16,800
Total	179	2,474,400

NINE

Small Indigenous Industry

POLICY DEBATES

FROM THE early 1970s until 1978, discussions at board level in the organisation focused more and more on avenues to development of a social as well as an economic nature. As early as 1974, the board noted that establishing industry dealt with only one aspect of regional problems and that other means of development needed to be reviewed, such as village renewal, farm-based tourism, entertainment, leader identification and subregional organisation. In 1975 the company was increasingly viewed as a force in total community development: future investments were seen in small industries and building holiday cottages for sale.

Much of the push for this approach came from Brendan O'Regan. He explained:

> There were many dimensions here – cultural development, small factory units – we wanted to give encouragement to natural leaders in each village, local leadership by individuals was the key, establish a network of local leaders.[1]

In 1976, the board agreed priority tasks in three categories:

1. Achievement of job target.
2. Fully shaping proposals and commencing actions for new company activities, specifically village renewal and rural action via holiday cottages for sale, and a proposed trade and exhibition centre at Shannon.
3. Air traffic development.

Brendan O'Regan's proposal

In June 1977, the board had another discussion on future directions, generating a suggestion that SFADCo should operate over the whole of the West of Ireland, but as a community development agency, giving up the industrial functions. This proposal was particularly associated with the chairman, Brendan O'Regan, and there was a considerable divergence of viewpoints and opinions here.

Brendan O'Regan believed that the special experience and insights of SFADCo could be of benefit to other regions planning for regional development in the forms of community-based tourism, physical development of villages, local enterprise and tourism entertainment. This suggestion implied that the company should now concentrate on these activities, transferring many of its industrial functions to other agencies. Michael Killeen of the IDA supported this recommendation. But Paul Quigley argued differently, emphasising that SFADCo was still behind in its longer term objectives: airport traffic was too low; the new town needed to develop; the industrial estate was below its optimum employment; the region was critically short of jobs. With scarce resources, carefully chosen priorities were critical, he claimed. However, it was Brendan O'Regan's view-point that prevailed at the meeting. Brendan O'Regan explained to the author: 'I wanted to give the company a mission it could call its own, something it could do uniquely better than other agencies.'[2]

Some weeks later, in October 1977, a letter was dispatched to Minister O'Malley setting out the board's recommendations. As SFADCo had special experience in the full economic and social development of villages and smaller communities, as well as filling gaps where there was no other agency to do so, it meant that SFADCo should concentrate on providing community activities and village amenities for tourists, creating conditions for the growth of crafts, and physical improvements to villages. To do this, SFADCo would give up the promotion of new industry. But Paul Quigley and his management team (in a note to the board) continued to argue against the board's decision, claiming that SFADCo needed to retain its regional industrial development functions and that nobody in government had suggested any of the suggested changes. The board's proposal had very negative staffing and organisational implications, and many of the actions they proposed could be secured within the present arrangement, according to Paul Quigley. The board had made little assessment of the existing situation, Paul Quigley believed.

Des O'Malley's response

The following month, in November 1977, the board met with Des O'Malley. His reaction to Brendan O'Regan's idea was negative. He responded that SFADCo should be more economically oriented than the proposal suggested, and that the agency should be given a task more

worthy of its abilities. There was a task of fundamental national importance
he saw for SFADCo – the development of indigenous Irish industry. He
envisaged a region being taken as a pilot area. Each parish and town would
be combed to uncover potential entrepreneurs. The Mid West, because it
had established a regional identity, was an obvious choice as a pilot area
and SFADCo existed there as a force to do the job.

Des O'Malley explained his thinking at the time:

> The closure of Ferenka was imminent with 1,700 jobs about to be
> lost. We had to switch the company's approach to respond effectively
> to the unemployment crisis. The initial proposals that came to me
> were too influenced by social–cultural considerations.[3]

The record of the meeting notes an enthusiastic reception to O'Malley's
proposal, both the board and management welcoming the new role.
However, Des O'Malley later commented: 'That was the official response
but there was some resistance at middle management level which was
overcome. Perhaps resistance is too strong a word and lack of enthusiasm
might be more accurate.'[4]

Two months later, in January 1978, Des O'Malley announced the new
direction for SFADCo. He did this when the Dáil met to debate the update
on the SFADCo legislation. O'Malley said that he was in consultations
with the SFADCo board with a view to giving a new dimension to their
work. He considered that the original objective – to secure the future of
Shannon Airport – had been substantially achieved and that the flair of the
organisation might be turned in a new direction.

O'Malley explained that the balance of Ireland's industrial structure
required that the country should seek to strengthen greatly the position of
indigenous Irish industry, especially small industry. He was therefore
suggesting that SFADCo:

> should assume responsibility for the development of small indigenous
> industry in the Mid West Region in a special and intensive way not
> hitherto attempted in this country. I see this as a pilot exercise, the
> results of which would be evaluated at the end of 18 months or two
> years where decisions would be taken about the extension of such an
> intensive drive to other regions.[5]

To free up SFADCo, and to strengthen overseas links, he was arranging for
the IDA to take over responsibility for other industry in the Mid West, and
to open an office in Limerick. O'Malley's desire for a regional pilot project

also arose from a concern not to change the operation of the IDA. The IDA, he said, were professionals and highly successful and he would not interfere with their activities in foreign industry. Therefore, he felt that the most successful regional organisation in the country, SFADCo, should be the one to spearhead an all-out effort to develop entrepreneurship among our own people. The extension of this experience to other areas could be done in a number of ways e.g. expand the operations of SFADCo outside the Mid West region, or second SFADCo staff to other areas.

Both deputies and senators accepted it, although some very grudgingly. Two main objections were raised in the ensuing debate. Firstly, the transfer of significant industrial functions from SFADCo to the IDA was seen by some as downgrading regional development – a move towards centralisation that would weaken SFADCo:

> It represents a complete contradiction of the modern concept of regional development and regional agencies ... the concept of regional development appears to have been scrapped totally'.[6]

Secondly, others thought that the relationship between SFADCo and IDA was becoming heavily complex and complicated:

> The Minister will finish up arbitrating between SFADCo and IDA. His predecessor had to do it and his predecessor's predecessor had to do it.[7]

SMALL INDUSTRY DEVELOPMENT

Following the O'Malley announcement, arrangements were put in hand to reorganise for the new role. For the subsequent two to three years, SFADCo was to become a hive of innovative activity and new schemes for small indigenous industry. Some of these first-time programmes are worth summarising here.

- A network of local field offices was established, one per county. Each aimed to act as an efficient and easily accessible small industry information centre for its particular area by harmonising support for small industry and processing local enquiries. A business services division was established to give management and technical advice to small industry in areas such as finance, marketing, production engineering, materials and purchasing. This was subsequently absorbed into the project appraisal system.

- Opportunities for subcontract and import–substitution were promoted. By acting as broker between large firms and small firms, SFADCo aimed to secure the fullest benefit from overseas sponsored investment by small industry. This was called the 'matchmaker' service. It aimed to match the products and services of small industry with the requirements of big industry, later becoming part of the 'national linkage programme'.
- Several series of publications were aimed at small industry in the form of periodic enterprise magazines and advisory and information guidelines.
- 'Youth Enterprise Shannon' was established to encourage employment and development projects stimulated by young people.
- A small industry innovation centre was developed on the campus of the National Institute of Higher Education (today the University of Limerick). The concept of this centre was to provide facilities to allow high technology small industry to incubate using the technical facilities of NIHE, as well as providing a technical research and development centre for small industry. The innovation centre was a unit within the organisation (without separate legal status) but its direction was delegated to a separate executive board on a somewhat informal basis. Apart from SFADCo, representation on this board was drawn from the IDA, NIHE, Institute for Industrial Research and Standards and the Department of Industry and Commerce.

The centre was substantially influenced by the experience of the invention centres in Denmark, focussing on two main strategies: sourcing of products for manufacture (joint ventures and licences) and development of inventions. The centre did go through a number of significant changes in goals during its early life. By the 1980s the centre was seen to be generating a substantial number of high quality potential projects, located throughout the country. The centre was increasingly seen as a national facility developing projects for both the Mid West and other regions, part of the national industrial development infrastructure. However, this view of the centre as a national service subsequently receded. Alternative and equivalent services developed in other regions and the centre has since been more closely integrated into the Mid West regional industrial support programmes.

Self–financing was an early goal of the centre. During the early 1980s, a target was set to achieve financial self-sufficiency by 1990, linked to a potential national role for the centre. However, by 1985 it was clear to many that the nature of the innovation centre's work was non-commercial: this did not allow for financial independence. In practical terms the innovation centre provided workshops, information resources and advisory and other schemes for new technology entrepreneurs. By the late 1980s, over 160 projects had been evaluated of which thirty-six had commenced trading and twenty of these were operational by 1991, employing over 400 people.

- A number of training programmes aimed at small business were developed, including courses on product development, starting your own business, book-keeping, credit control, financial administration, business management marketing and others. Between one and two hundred people participated each year. One significant feature of these courses was that they all involved very close collaboration with other agencies e.g. AnCo, Irish Productivity Centre, Irish Management Institute and others. This collaboration seems almost to have been invisible with relatively smooth cooperation between the partners. Many of these programmes later absorbed subsequently into the private sector or AnCo.

- A graduates in industry programme was developed to place engineering and marketing graduates in small industries for eighteen months, aiming to provide graduates with useful experience and to inject expertise into small firms. The programmes for engineering and marketing were initiated with the Institute for Industrial Research and Standards and Coras Trachtala respectively. These innovations developed into national programmes through those two bodies.

- A small industry factory building programme resulted in the completion of enterprise centres, workspace centres and business centres. There was considerable experimentation with new forms of factory provision. In 1978–81 over 200 factory units were completed covering over 50,000 square metres, relatively dispersed in over forty separate locations. New approaches were tested in many cases such as different rental arrangements, variations in space standards, shared services and other features. The name enterprise centre was brought into use. SFADCo executives disliked the earlier term of incubation centre.

- The Microelectronics Application Centre (MAC) was established in 1979. This was a cooperative venture between SFADCo, NIHE, IDA and the National Board for Science and Technology. The objective of MAC was to help Irish firms take maximum advantage of the ongoing microprocessor revolution, with the hope that MAC would be self-financing in a few years. MAC worked to promote the use of microelectronics technology in Irish industry through a contract design and development service. By 1981, it was a nationwide service and constituted as a separate company. However, by 1984, trading difficulties were being experienced and significant losses were reported. Certainly, the short-term outcome did not meet the original high expectations. Consequently, MAC was restructured and slimmed down to a scale more appropriate to its level of business. MAC survived and later developed into a commercial state company with 200 consultancy projects to its name.

- Food and natural resources also attracted significant attention during the course of the small industry programme. For example, in 1978, a joint venture was agreed between SFADCo and a commercial operator to establish Shannon Nurseries, a brokerage for the purchase and sale of hardy nursery stock. The concept was for a marketing and distribution unit to organise and coordinate the wide range of small independent nursery stock producers. The idea was welcomed by many involved. By 1983, the Shannon Nursery project was noted to have been successful in improving the structure of the market and in raising the technical competence of growers. However, substantial trading losses were also being reported, arising from insufficient share capital and heavy borrowing. Subsequently, a reconstruction package was put in place and the financial situation of Shannon Nurseries improved. But difficulties with the enterprise would continue to cause concern.

- Several other initiatives were taken to stimulate small industry in the food sector. A food and drink exhibition was organised in 1982, together with a conference on food processing.

- A regional food centre was opened in Limerick in 1984. This provided factory space built to the international standards of quality and hygiene demanded in the world food industry in the form of units for small-scale food firms. The food centre also incorporated an experimental food kitchen for testing new food products. An agribusiness programme was launched aimed at developing integrated projects in primary production and processing e.g. deer, geese, pheasant and others. In 1984, the Government's White Paper on Industrial Policy announced a 'pilot project for the development of the food processing sector' by SFADCo.

- An urban renewal project was initiated at the granary in Limerick City, a disused Georgian warehouse occupying a prominent site in the centre. SFADCo, in conjunction with Limerick Corporation, purchased a limited option on the building and devised a restoration and development scheme for it. The project proposal was then successfully introduced to a private sector investor.

The overall small industry programme had a significant impact on development.

FIGURE 28

SMALL INDIGENOUS INDUSTRY IN THE MID WEST REGION[8]

Year	1977	1982	1987
Enterprises	298	564	635
Jobs	2,986	3,747	4,463

During the first five years of the programme, the numbers of enterprises almost doubled and this was seen to be evidence of an entrepreneurial climate in the region. However, numbers employed in these new enterprises were small, and relatively dependent on domestic markets and low levels of technology. See Figure 28.

The results of the small industry programme were reviewed by the Oireachtas in 1980.[9] Des O'Malley was expansive: 'I can now tell the House that the experiment was successful.' He explained that a two pronged strategy had been adopted by SFADCo. One strategy was to bring out the full potential of small indigenous industry through direct assistance to small-scale start-ups and expansions. The second strategy was to devise and test new ideas to stimulate the growth of native small industry. O'Malley went on to outline the outcome of both these strategies – the results of development on the ground in terms of jobs and projects, and the various innovative programmes that had been launched.

Response from both Houses was very enthusiastic, with members applauding the direction now being followed. There was some discussion about methods to transfer the results to other regions, O'Malley reported that he would see a somewhat re-jigged regional IDA organisation as being the most suitable way to do it. However, more critical comment came from the Industrial Policy Review of 1982.[10] The review claimed that the direction of the SFADCo pilot project was towards intense 'hands-on consulting'. The review questioned this approach, doubting that it was an effective long-term means for the development of skills and exports. It had, according to the review, the effect of increasing the dependence of small firms on outside services, instead of stimulating in-house solutions or cross-company initiatives. The review argued that a major push towards skill development and competitiveness needed the building of in-house capabilities within small firms, rather than a 'never-ending provision of consultancy services'.

INNOVATION IN ORGANISATIONS

What happened in SFADCo between 1978 and the early 1980s was a demonstrable example of innovation in an organisation. The volume of new measures introduced was considerable – field offices, innovation centre, Microelectronics Application Centre and others. A term coined to express this type of activity has been 'intrapreneurship' i.e. enterprise within organisations.[11] The causes of this upsurge of intrapreneurship and the factors stimulating this growth in innovative activity deserve to be investigated. Presumably, if these factors can be illuminated, their discovery can give us general ideas about enterprise in organisations.

Affecting the emergence of new ideas for small industry development are factors both external and internal to the agency. The environment external to SFADCo contained both opportunities and threats to the company. A significant opportunity was that development thinking at the time was experiencing a strong swing towards the idea of small business, both the Birch Study in the US and the Bolton Report in the UK bringing the issue of small industry to the national agenda in both countries. There were a lot of ideas around – advisory services to small business; financing small business; the physical environment for small business and management aspects. SFADCo, as an early player in the field of small industry develop-ment, was therefore in an excellent position to capitalise on these emerging concepts. There was much that could be learnt.

A further opportunity was the existence of considerable national impetus for the project. For example, Des O'Malley clearly indicated that this regional pilot project in small industry development had national implications, giving a boost to the venture. But it also contained elements of threat in that O'Malley intimated that 'decisions' would be taken after 1980 about the outcome of the project. The anecdotal evidence suggests that this was taken to mean that the credibility, and future, of the agency would be at stake, depending on the results of the small industry programme. Such a scenario concentrated minds wonderfully!

But minds were not just being concentrated at SFADCo. There is evidence that the IDA experienced a new-found interest in small industry at the same time. O'Malley explained in the Dáil:

> The IDA have now achieved a situation where one third of their job approvals are for small Irish industry and there is within that organisation a new enthusiasm for the possibilities which exist. It is understandable that in the past some people in the IDA might have

thought that the larger and more spectacular projects providing large numbers of jobs, using spectacular technology and heavier investment, were more attractive. I am happy to say that the perception is certainly wrong.[12]

There has been some anecdotal suggestions that the existence of the regional pilot project, and the possibility of its extension elsewhere, may have spurred the IDA to greater effort in small industry. For example, there was some discussion during 1980 about a possible extension of SFADCo functions outside the Mid West but Michael Killeen of the IDA argued against this. He reported that IDA were putting proposals to the Minister about small industry development throughout the country, and that he did not envisage the extension of SFADCo to other areas: it would produce instability and wasteful competition, he felt. But the stated possibility of extending SFADCo to IDA areas may well have generated thoroughly productive rivalries between the two agencies, as they tried to outperform each other in achievement.

How did Des O'Malley perceive this? Did he actually foment such rivalry for national policy purposes? O'Malley confirmed this to be true:

The short answer is yes. It worked. Within six months of Shannon Development starting, IDA had reorganised themselves. They strengthened their regional offices.[13]

O'Malley explained that IDA had paid lip service to small industry development before 1978. It was not possible to organise a small industry programme from Dublin. But by the time the Shannon Development programme was completed in 1981, IDA had strong regional structures in place: 'Shannon Development had the effect of provoking IDA into doing something about small industry they had not done before.'[14]

These sets of external threats and opportunities were complemented by factors within the organisation. There is informal evidence that such internal factors played a prominent role. Firstly, the apparent reputation of the agency for innovative approaches to development provided a spur for renewed effort and vigour. Organisational culture and self-image had an innovatory bias, harking back to the 1960s, providing a strong motive for change. Secondly, as a regional agency, it seems that personal contact, networks and local knowledge were relatively strong within the organisation, accelerating learning and response to industrial customers. A third internal factor was the emergence of internal unity within the company between board and management. The earlier period 1974–78 had been marked by some differences of opinion between Brendan O'Regan's board and Paul Quigley's management team, culminating in the internal debate about future directions in 1977. However, the resolution offered by Des O'Malley unified the different views. Paul Quigley confirmed this, saying that in 1978 after a long period of internal differences: 'The executive and board were at one on what policies and actions were needed.'[15]

This internal unity and common purpose formed a vital third ingredient in the success of the 1978–83 small indigenous industry programme. Concluding, therefore, on a general level, the SFADCo pilot project in small industry highlights general issues about intrapreneurship on an organisation-wide scale. The lessons are that external factors of threats and opportunities and internal conditions of organisational culture lined up, complementing each other. Each group of factors reinforced the other – a clearly perceived set of external factors, strong internal agreement on goals, moral purpose and vision within the agency, complemented by external support and opportunities, with an element of threat.

The general statement would thus be that organisational innovation flows best when three conditions are satisfied at the one time:

- Significant external opportunity.
- Some element of threat.
- Clear perception and strong motivation within the enterprise.

The suggestion is that organisational innovation comes in waves. The strength and timing of these surges depends on a fortuitous combination of circumstances, and it is when these factors come together that we see a rising swell of intrapreneurship.

TEN

Organisation and Finance

STRATEGY AND STRUCTURE

THE EVOLUTION of strategy in SFADCo would undoubtedly have caused changes in the organisation's structure. But the organisation itself may well have influenced its own strategic make up: thus its objectives and approach to the task would also have been affected by the organisational arrangements. Structure and strategy are interdependent, acting on each other. One simple evolution of organisational structure has been highlighted in the literature,[1] involving the growth of the organisation through three types of structures:

* Functional
* Multidivisional
* Holding company

Initially it has been noted that organisations follow a functional structure – the firm is organised around one business with a simple hierarchy of functions. SFADCo's structure reflected this, with all major units reporting directly to the chief executive during the 1960s. See Figure 29.

Organisations tend to evolve from the functional type to the multidivisional type. Decentralisation increases in the organisation with different units growing in self-containment in a system of mutual interdependence.

FIGURE 29

SFADCO ORGANISATION, 1967

General manager	◄	Developments
	◄	Central planning
	◄	Publicity and aviation
	◄	Tourism
	◄	Industrial promotion
	◄	Company secretary

143

FIGURE 30

SFADCO ORGANISATION, 1970

	◄———	Physical Resources Group
General Manager	◄———	Planning & Promotion Group
	◄———	Finance & Administration Group

This happened at SFADCo as the increasing size and complexity of the organisation dictated the need for new structures. See Figure 30.

But while SFADCo evolved from a functional to a multidivisional structure, it never developed into the third category of 'holding company'. The latter category represents a further stage of organisational decentralisation, with central headquarters making purely financial decisions about independently managed units. SFADCo retained almost all its functions within the main organisation, and never became like that. However, there were three cases where SFADCo developed new support programmes at arm's length, using a shareholding or loan arrangement:

- Rent an Irish Cottage (21% shares).
- Shannon Nurseries (39% shares).
- Microelectronics Applications Centre (loan).

In these cases, the SFADCo relationship to these three units would have approached some elements of the holding company model. But it is significant that, in all three cases, there were trading difficulties. In the case of Rent an Irish Cottage and Shannon Nurseries these were severe, lasting a considerable length of time. In the case of the Microelectronics Application Centre (MAC) losses were very significant, but more short-term. All involved substantial restructuring. The reasons for these difficulties deserve discussion. Some might argue that the existence of such difficulties demonstrates that the public sector has no business in commercial enterprises, citing these cases as examples. But others would counter that by pointing to the novelty of the ventures and their necessary strategic significance to the sectors which they supported i.e. upgrading village tourism, opening opportunities for nursery producers and exposing industry to microelectronic technology.

There is another explanation, arising from the organisational setting. Galbraith and Nathanson have argued that, for new product development, the holding company is an inadequate structure.[2] For new ventures, management needs to be fully informed, keep abreast of information and learn about the new business. The argument, therefore, is that new products and programmes need to be developed within the structure of the parent organisation and should not be decentralised to a subsidiary before approaching maturity. By this time, management should be aware of the eccentricities of the new venture. The interesting point about Rent an Irish Cottage, Shannon Nurseries and the MAC is that they all represent new products in new subsidiaries, and all ran into difficulties. The management issue is significant. Board minutes at SFADCo record concerns about the management of all three. Placing these emerging ventures in a subsidiary-type structure distanced SFADCo's management from these programmes just when they needed to be closest with hands-on control. Ironically, SFADCo had very good motivations for using the holding company approach. It conformed to successive national policy guidelines which dictated that a state development company should distance itself from commercial activity. Also, the establishment of separate companies permitted direct partnership with the private sector. Paul Quigley remarked: 'It helped establish support from other public bodies whose interest was essential – university, local authorities, IDA.'[3]

But, whatever the motivation, this approach meant the breaking of a golden rule about not having new products in new subsidiaries. As a result, management in SFADCo were one step removed from day-to-day issues of the new projects, at the very time when tight control was most necessary. This involved the company in some troublesome rescues, thus paying a price. The general argument here is that development corporations are in a role-conflict, distancing themselves from commercial activity while simultaneously exercising effective management. There are considerable difficulties in reconciling these separate tasks.

BUREAUCRATISATION?

A suggestion by researchers is that the growth of an organisation brings with it internal social change. For example, some writers[4] suggest that organisations experience a shift of emphasis from ends to means. They pay increasingly more attention to the rules and regulations rather than to the original objectives, a process called bureaucratisation. The extent to which this can be observed in SFADCo invites study.

Change in manpower structures may be useful here. Between the mid-1960s and mid-1970s the organisation was considerably transformed. Figure 31 illustrates this transformation in terms of staff numbers in various categories:

FIGURE 31

SFADCO STAFF BY CATEGORY (%)[5]

Category	1965	1975
Administration**	16	20
Property	38	39
Industry	11	17
Tourism/Air Traffic	20	9
Publicity	13	10
Research	2	5
Total	100	100
(Actual Numbers)	(87)	(191)

** General management, administration, finance, personnel

Total staff numbers doubled over this period, a reflection of the additional tasks of regional industrial development.

There was some increase in the share of administration staff, but this was probably to be expected with the changing structure from functional to multidivisional. Significantly the property sector did not increase in share of total staff. This could be important, given the fact that SFADCo's property (both housing and industry) expanded substantially at this time. One might have expected an increasing share of property related staff. The most rapidly growing categories were in industry and research – their combined share went from 13% to 22% over the period, reflecting the increased regional orientation. The conclusion is thus there was nothing in the formal division of labour that reinforced bureaucratisation. The administration and property sectors did not enlarge substantially in their share of staff numbers.

A further factor influencing bureaucratisation is the number of grades, or levels, in the organisation: increasing internal differentiation brings with it demarcation and more hierarchy. The trends in SFADCo are worth examination. Figure 32 presents the number of staff and grades:

FIGURE 32

SFADCO STAFF AND GRADES[6]

Year	Staff	No. of grades
1965	82	11
1975	191	16

The table above would suggest that while staff numbers more than doubled in the organisation, the number of grades grew far less sharply. Thus increases in staff volumes were not necessarily accompanied by greater demarcation. The conclusion in this case would be that there was no evidence of bureaucratisation arising specifically from changes in the internal formal organisation of the agency.

FINANCIAL ASPECTS

SFADCo's financing was initially in direct grants from the exchequer. These grants were of three types:

1. Grants towards running expenses of the company, both administration and promotion.
2. Grants to industry, both at Shannon (via the exchequer) and in the Mid West Region (via the IDA).
3. Support towards housing subsidies at Shannon, which were repayable to the exchequer out of rents.

In addition, SFADCo received an allocation for capital expenditure (industry and tourism) in the form of share capital contributed by the exchequer.

Over the years, the structure of SFADCo income and expenditure changed considerably. As the company's property portfolio increased, so too did rental income. The company retained this to finance its own running expenses and by 1970, self-generated income was equalling 70% of running expenses. Thus SFADCo was 'self-financing' to a considerable extent, although this was not self-financing in a strictly commercial sense. The company did not surrender factory rents to the exchequer to repay the cost of capital used in construction of those factories but was allowed to retain this income to finance its own operating expenses. This is shown in Figure 34.

There was a considerable change in the way in which exchequer allocations were approached. The early years were a much easier period for SFADCo and Peter Donnelly reported:

> By and large we did very well. The annual budget approved by the board would be agreed with the Department of Industry and Commerce, and we would then help the department argue the case

with the Department of Finance. It was all very gentlemanly and friendly. But after the Lemass era, the attitude of the civil servants began to change and they became less positive towards Shannon.[7]

This shift in attitude was brought about by a number of factors. Change in the personal contact network was undoubtedly one of them, as Peter Donnelly pointed out. But there were others too: the entire country was industrialising and pressure on the public purse was mounting. The civil servants had to mediate between increasing and conflicting claims on public finances and SFADCo inevitably found it more and more difficult to secure the financial support from the exchequer that it perceived necessary. This is illustrated graphically in Figure 33, which shows how SFADCo capital and grants expenditure, expressed as a percentage of the industrial public capital programme, declined substantially.

FIGURE 33

SFADCO FINANCE (£000, CURRENT PRICES)

Category	1960	1965	1970	1975	1980	1985
Income						
Grants						
• running expenses	99	–	415	1,140	1,402	4,491
• grants to industry	56	480	856	1,689	4,992	5,665
• housing advances	–	28	77	247	437	400
Self-generated	3	134	367	1,253	3,385	6,509
Total income	158	642	1,715	4,329	10,216	17,065
Expenditure						
Operating						
• running expenses/ promotion	61	268	491	1,646	4,145	9,108
• grants to industry	56	208	856	1,689	4,744	6,328
• housing repayments	0	185	338	986	1,203	1,404
Total operating	117	661	1,685	4,321	10,092	16,840
Capital expenditure	294	934	3,864	6,223	14,846	7,296
Total expenditure	411	1,595	5,549	10,544	24,938	24,136

FIGURE 34
SFADCO AND NATIONAL EXPENDITURE[8]

Year	Public Capital Programme (Industry)	SFADCo Capital/Grants Expenditure	SFADCo as % of Public Capital Programme
1960	£2.8m	£0.4m	14%
1965	£7.4m	£1.1m	15%
1970	£20.2m	£4.7m	23%
1975	£61.6m	£7.9m	13%
1980	£324.0m	£19.6m	6%
1985	£346.0m	£13.6m	4%

ELEVEN

Different Interpretations

THIS REVIEW of twenty eight years of SFADCo, its policies and strategies, has highlighted different evaluations and interpretations of the organisation. If we look at the comments made of the company, we can classify them in two ways: whether they are made from a national or a regional perspective, and whether they are positive or negative. We can therefore divide the interpretations into four schools of thought:

- National perspective/positive view: SFADCo is a specialist organisation, implementing a project of national significance in one locality.
- Regional perspective/positive view: SFADCo is a generalist regional organisation, integrating diverse strands of development in a coordinated manner ('development from below').
- National perspective/negative view: SFADCo duplicates national programmes, overlaps excessively with other agencies and complicates an already enlarged public service.
- Regional perspective/negative view: SFADCo is remote from its own region and the people in it.

NATIONAL PROJECT, LOCALLY DRIVEN

The view that SFADCo was an organisation with a specific national task, pursued in one local area, was first voiced by Erskine Childers in the 1959 Dáil debate. Childers argued that SFADCo was to make Shannon Airport unique as an industrial area. He said that it would be impossible for other agencies to become Shannon specialists, and take the specialised approach that was necessary. The whole basis of SFADCo, he felt, was that it was a company that would specialise entirely in developing Shannon Airport and all this could not be done mechanically by central organisations.

Although this was a view much challenged at the time, the success of Shannon in the 1960s reinforced this particular perception. SFADCo's regional development involvement in the 1970s also drew support on the basis of its national impact. For example, Minister Justin Keating argued in the Senate in March 1978 that regional development programmes like SFADCo's had positive national consequences. This was in terms of counteracting the growth of Dublin. Keating claimed that other places need to grow more rapidly than Dublin and that they need to grow past the threshold point where they can sustain all the things that people near modern cities are entitled to. Keating claimed that SFADCo's role was to develop the Limerick/Shannon area on a scale that would thus counterbalance Dublin.

The potential national impact of SFADCo was further echoed by Keating's successor, Minister Des O'Malley. In the Dáil in 1978, he announced the new small industry programme, seeing this as a pilot exercise, not hitherto attempted in this country and one that could be extended (by SFADCo or others) to other regions. O'Malley was pointing here to an important national function of the organisation – that of innovation, experimentation and pilot testing programmes for national application later.

This idea of the national impact of SFADCo was taken up by Paul Quigley in 1987. In a conference paper following his retirement, Paul Quigley claimed that there were important informal national consequences to do with competition in the public sector. Quigley argued that SFADCo's greatest contribution to national development was not in innovation, traffic, tourism, small industry development, regional development, town building, urban development or practical planning but in a form of 'monopoly-breaking'.

> SFADCo provided comparisons with, and generated competition in enterprise with, other national agencies each of which would otherwise be alone in its own field. And to be alone in its field, for a state agency, is to be a form of monopoly, with all the dangers of cosy self-satisfaction which that implies. It must be a nuisance to the IDA and to Bord Fáilte to have another agency engaged in industrial development and in tourism; but it is, like private enterprise's inescapable need to be profitable, the sort of nuisance that leads to better performance and greater efficiency all round.[1]

Because SFADCo was doing the same things that were being done elsewhere by other agencies, but often doing them differently, and sometimes being ahead of them in initiatives and in results, and sometimes being under them in costs, it gave ministers and civil servants comparative data of great value both towards policy formation and towards control. It was of tremendous benefit for a minister to be able to test and compare different approaches, and to do so on a limited basis without deflecting from major national strategies, according to Paul Quigley.

The comfort of monopoly situations was tempting, and once or twice in the past other agencies have lent support to those who were pushing centralising processes that would reduce SFADCo's scope and functions, or so Paul Quigley said. But he felt that really good managers welcomed competition, of whatever sort, and disliked monopolies and generally the relationship between the bodies was an excellent one, built on mutual respect. Des O'Malley's comment that Shannon Development provoked the IDA into doing more for small industry illustrates this point.

Significantly, Paul Quigley's theory attracts some international academic support. Commentators[2] argued that government regulation of the economy (including its agencies) is difficult to analyse. The regulatory bodies (such as government departments) are often ill-equipped and underfunded to regulate the entities they seek to monitor. The entities being regulated, such as public organisations or private sector producers, are frequently more financially powerful, with greater resources, than the regulatory bodies. They often thwart the efforts of the regulators and there is a danger that the regulatory body may be 'captured'. These organisations frequently condition or dilute the thinking of the officials who are supposed to be doing the regulating.

Perhaps Paul Quigley, with his arguments about SFADCo's contribution to competition in the public service, has produced a solution to this quandary: regulation through comparison. The Quigley viewpoint would argue that rivalry and friendly competition between agencies makes it easier for government to supervise and regulate them. Competition in the public sector can thus be functional for public policy and public interests.

'DEVELOPMENT FROM BELOW'

Another, and related, view of SFADCo is that it serves a function as a generalist regional organisation, integrating diverse strands of development in a coordinated manner. The argument is that this approach generates and sustains better development than a more centralist approach by national specialist agencies.

Speaking in 1978, Paul Quigley argued that there are real advantages in organising for development on an area or regional basis, as distinct from simply on a basis of functions:

> Confinement of such components in watertight functional compartments can have useful advantages, such as greater scope for the development of professional expertise; but it can have serious disadvantages also. Economic or social life does not confine itself to such compartments and neither should the instruments to improve them be over-compartmentalised.[3]

Paul Quigley also claimed that the location within regions of power to act on key components of regional development may necessarily involve untidy administration which overlaps, or even competes with, agencies funded from the same national purse. Administrators, very naturally, dislike untidy organisational arrangements. But Paul Quigley stated it could be a much better thing than the present strong, central control that embraces all state agencies in a single monolithic structure.

> Organisational individuality is fundamental for enterprise and initiative; and to diminish it for the sake of tidy solutions and ready controls may cost the nation a great deal more than seems to be generally recognised.[4]

Single function agencies operating nation-wide, like the IDA and the Irish Tourist Board, had a great deal to be said for them, according to Paul Quigley. They could act uniformly and fairly throughout the country, as justice and practical politics require. The fact that there was a single voice on a given subject means they could afford very high levels of expertise. And they had available the possibilities of economies of scale.

> But their specialisation has drawbacks, too. In the real world many development needs and opportunities do not fall into neat categories of industry promotion or export promotion or tourism or whatever. And those things which do fall mainly into such categories often spill out of them to quite a significant extent. SFADCo's multi-functional nature gave it a perception of the interdependence of different sectors. The organisation thus had an ability to respond to opportunities that would not have been grasped so readily by specialist single function units.[5]

Paul Quigley's perspective attracted particular support from two OECD publications. A manpower study by OECD observers in 1974 argued that the achievements of SFADCo illustrated the advantages of a regional planning organisation based on a strong central unit coordinating and managing local programmes. OECD felt that it was in touch with local conditions and requirements, able to pull together the different strands of local development and willing to take initiatives to achieve the results it required. A later OECD study in 1987 claimed that the experience in the Mid West region constituted a useful precedent for the successful conduct of the decentralisation process and for the creation of conditions for promoting innovation and setting up new firms. OECD acknowledged that:

> The cost of the Shannon experience has been high and some of its initiatives could be questioned. However, it is undeniable that a new climate has been created in the region, characterised by a remarkable entrepreneurial dynamism. This is manifest not only in technology and industry in a narrow sense, but also in renovation of towns, adaptation of Shannon Airport services, and development of cultural activities.[6]

Tom Barrington argued that Ireland is highly centralised, compared to other European countries, thus creating problems with local coordination of services. He pointed to SFADCo as an example of effective local integration.[7]

Paul Quigley, Tom Barrington and the OECD researchers share a common theory that decentralised policies of regional development potentially produce higher absolute levels of economic growth, so the whole nation benefits.

DUPLICATION

While the foregoing were positive perspectives on the organisation, a number of significant criticisms were also made. One of these criticisms was that the existence and actions of SFADCo introduced excessive bureaucratic complexities and cut across clearly defined national programmes, creating confusion.

At the Dáil debate in 1959, James Dillon was scathing at the apparent subdivision of grant-giving powers between several agencies. Dillon argued that there should only be one national grant giving authority. Allowing grant-giving powers to a local agency like SFADCo, as well as the national agency, complicated matters: 'Do I perceive here the inauguration of the operation of Parkinson's Law?'[8] During the 1960s this viewpoint receded as the development successes at Shannon during that decade satisfied any arguments about administrative coordination. However, by the late 1960s, the opinion that SFADCo was complicating matters was definitely back, this time with a vengeance.

In August, 1968, R.C. O'Connor of Aer Rianta argued that his body, the National Airports Authority, should have complete control of all airports, taking over all SFADCo functions in relation to the airport – sales and catering, aviation promotion and publicity. Two years later, in 1970, Michael Killeen of the IDA claimed that all regions of the country should receive the same treatment under the industrial development legislation: the same operational procedures, the same criteria for assessment of projects and the same formula for grant payments. This meant that consistency of approach was vital and that SFADCo should only have delegation equivalent to a local IDA office.

Apart from chief executives of other state agencies, officials of government departments were also raising similar issues. In 1973, Department of Transport officials argued that doubt existed as to whether SFADCo was the appropriate body to promote Shannon. Circumstances had changed, they said, and funds allocated to SFADCo seemed to be spent in the narrow interests of Shannon. Perhaps the Irish Tourist Board should be doing this in the interests of the country as a whole, they suggested. In 1978, Barry Desmond in the Dáil pointed to the multiplicity of organisations in the Mid West, claiming that these activities should be more effectively coordinated. Perhaps SFADCo should be subsumed within the national structures of the IDA and Aer Rianta.

In 1985, the Dáil Committee on Public Expenditure examined SFADCo. The committee acknowledged that the company had a significant impact on regional development. But the committee's report did refer to questions of overlapping and duplication, and the issue of assigning some of SFADCo's functions to national bodies. The committee felt that many of these functions should be transferred to the appropriate national bodies, so that SFADCo could concentrate on the specialist task of 'regional development' (although the committee did not clearly specify what this meant). In sum, the theory that SFADCo overlaps or duplicates or complicates smooth national programmes was a very popular one, with absolutely no shortage of adherents!

REMOTE FROM PEOPLE

Within the region, SFADCo attracted its share of criticism. The archives suggest three areas where such critique arose.

- Firstly, in Shannon Town there were a number of cases of conflict between SFADCo and local residents. This arose particularly over rental issues and was conditioned by the landlord/tenant relationship, and the strongly dominant position of SFADCo, particularly during the 1960s. For example, one resident reported to researcher Liam Ryan: 'People complain not so much that Big Brother is watching but that Big Brother isn't even listening'.

- A second area of conflict was with regional communities over industrial location policy in the 1970s. Representatives of many areas, such as North Tipperary, argued that SFADCo policies excessively concentrated industries in the strong centres, reflecting a tension that continuously affected SFADCo/local authority relations during that decade.

- A third area of conflict within the region was reported by one significant political figure. He argued that the 'SFADCo whizz kids' had, by their perceived success, commandeered a large proportion of public funds towards Shannon and away from areas of need. There was also, he believed, overemphasis on self-image and public relations to the detriment of real action. This view was shared by a number of other political representatives.

In an interview, Fr Harry Bohan provided some strident criticism. Fr Bohan was consultant on human affairs with SFADCo (1968–80) and a member of the board of directors (1985–89). He pointed out that the early years of SFADCo were typified by getting the ideas first, and putting the structure on them afterwards. In later years, however, he argued that the opposite happened: SFADCo went through a period of being a structure without ideas, particularly in the sphere of regional industrial development.

> The big question was whether SFADCo were involved in regional development or industrial location. SFADCo did not seriously look at the resources of the region or the needs of rural areas. It got locked into industrial development instead of regional development. Once overseas industry stopped coming it did not know what to do.[9]

Fr Bohan argued that the staff did not make an effective transfer to the world of small industry, and continued to be imbued with the culture of big industry. He claimed that regional development strategies were radically different from industrial location strategies – different skills and approaches:

SFADCo got locked into a myth – too much money spent on PR, too little spent on research, not enough thinking. SFADCo did not want to believe that industry was not flowing in.[10]

A further problem highlighted by Fr Bohan was that SFADCo, being a monopoly force in the region, did not effectively partner with others: 'getting the credit was always the big issue for them'.

Further criticisms were voiced by Des O'Malley. O'Malley served as Minister for Industry and Commerce, 1977–81, with the company under his remit. O'Malley also represented a local constituency. These two facts thus brought him into frequent and intensive contact with the agency. On a number of occasions, Des O'Malley redirected SFADCo policies, particularly in encouraging developments away from Shannon, and into small industry promotion. Des O'Malley observed:

> A feature of Shannon Development in relation to any changes whatever has always been its institutional anxiety not to be interfered with from outside. In all Irish public bodies such as this there is a strong sense of institutional self-preservation which sometimes goes so far as to put the welfare of the organisation before the achievement of its tasks.[11]

These four viewpoints represent different organisational doctrines or development ideologies. A simple way of classifying them would be as follows:

FIGURE 35

CLASSIFICATION OF DEVELOPMENT IDEOLOGIES

Attitude	National Perspective	Regional Perspective
Positive	National project, locally driven	Development from below
Negative	Duplication	Remote from people

In many cases they reflect the assumptions, experiences and interests of the viewer. They appear at different times and at different strengths throughout the history of the organisation, arising both from individual perceptions and changing social and economic conditions.

TWELVE

Economic Impact

LOOKING at SFADCo over 1957–85, a period of two and a half decades, it is appropriate to examine the economic impact of the organisation and the additional effect of its presence. This question of the relative impact of a regional programme is a significant one. There is an argument that the key to alleviating high unemployment is through national policy measures, such as incentives, subsidies, labour force measures, support for output, provision of infrastructure and reduction of the costs of doing business. There would be a view that the key to employment growth is through such national measures, and that regional programmes have only a distracting effect, adding little to national output. For countries with an overall national unemployment problem, the question is about the relative effect of regional programmes and their contribution to national employment growth.

With SFADCo the issue is to define additional employment growth due to its presence, above and beyond that due to the impact of national policies (which would have happened anyway without the presence of the agency). One approach to answer this question would be compare employment in the Mid West with the national average. According to the Census of Population, the following were the Mid West and national employment trends for manufacturing industry:

FIGURE 36

EMPLOYMENT TRENDS IN THE MID WEST AND IRELAND[1]

Area	Employment in manufacturing			
	1961	1986	Change	% change
Mid West	10,747	21,678	+10,931	+102%
Ireland	179,436	215,283	+35,847	+20%

Figure 37 shows that growth in the Mid West was significantly ahead of the national average.

However, there are a number of reasons why a comparison between the Mid West and the Irish average is limited in its usefulness. The problem is that this Irish average is an amalgamation of several regions, and that there were national regional policies in operation in several specific regions, such as the Mid West.

During the 1960s and 1970s the Irish government adopted a sustained programme to direct new industrial investment away from Dublin towards the Western seaboard, including among other regions, the Mid West. In addition, high levels of grants to industry were offered along the Western seaboard, relative to the East. These were national measures that would have stimulated growth rates in the Mid West higher than the national average. Thus, although delivered locally by SFADCo, the outcome of these measures could not be attributed specifically to the existence of a local agency: local offices of national bodies could have done the same.

An alternative approach is to compare and contrast the employment outcome between the Mid West and the adjacent regions on the Western seaboard, i.e., Cork/Kerry and Galway/Mayo. Using the average employment change (1961–86) for the adjacent regions as a frame of reference for the Mid West has three particular merits. Firstly, the starting base in terms of general socio-economic conditions was similar between the Mid West and adjacent regions. The proportion of population living in urban as opposed to rural areas, and employed in agriculture as opposed to industry was broadly similar in 1961 between the Mid West and the adjacent regions. Secondly, both the Mid West and the Galway/Mayo and Cork/Kerry regions were subject to identical national policy measures, i.e., they benefited from the diversion of industry away from Dublin, and all contained designated areas offering relatively high grants to industry.

Thirdly, however, the Mid West was different from adjacent regions in that it had its own development agency whereas industrial and tourism development in Cork/Kerry and Galway/Mayo was promoted by local offices of national bodies, such as the IDA or the Irish Tourist Board (with the exception of the Irish-speaking districts under Udaras na Gaeltachta). Thus the Mid West can be viewed as the 'experiment' area (where a regional development programme was mounted) and the adjacent regions represent the 'control' area which was similar in many respects, except for the absence of a development agency. Presumably, if there are significant differences in the employment trends between the experimental and control areas, then those may be attributable to the presence of the development programme in the experimental area and its absence in the control area. The result could thus teach us something about the relative impact of regional development programmes as compared to national policy measures.

Details of employment trends for the Mid West and the adjacent regions are set out in Figures 38 and 39. They are given for twenty separate industrial groups, ranging over agriculture, manufacturing and services.

Overall, employment growth in the Mid West was only 4% between 1961 and 1986, and 7% in the adjacent regions. This sluggish growth was caused by a heavy downturn in agricultural employment, over 50% drop in both areas, just counterbalanced by growth in the non-agricultural sector.

In the non-agricultural sector, there were seven industrial groups where similar gains were achieved in both areas:

- Textile manufacture.
- Wood manufacture.
- Glass/cement.
- Construction.
- Commerce.
- Public administration.
- Professional services.

These are all industrial groups whose growth is not specifically targeted by public policy and a similar outcome for both the Mid West and adjacent areas could be expected. Three industrial groups showed better performance in the adjacent regions than in the Mid West:

- Food manufacture.
- Personal services.
- Other industries.

The growth of the food sector is explained by specific food companies in Kerry and Cork. Personal services (including domestic service) represented a lower rate of decline in the adjacent regions, although not substantially. The 'other industries' difference was large in percentage terms but not so much in absolute volumes.

Significantly, there were five industrial groups where growth in the Mid West substantially exceeded growth in the adjacent areas:

- Chemicals.
- Metals/electronics.
- Electricity.
- Insurance/business services.
- Transport.

FIGURE 37

EMPLOYMENT IN THE MID WEST REGION, 1961–86[2]

Industrial group	1961	1986	Change	% Change
Agriculture/forestry/fishing	44,630	20,581	−24,049	−54
Mining/extractive	332	402	+70	0
Manufacturing				
Food	3,976	3,541	−435	−11
Beverage/tobacco	346	343	−3	0
Textiles/clothing/footwear/ leather	2,278	1,307	−971	−43
Wood/wood products	823	1,320	+497	+60
Paper and printing	400	672	+272	+68
Chemical/rubber/plastic products	422	2,399	+1,977	+468
Glass/pottery/cement	755	1,806	+1,051	+139
Metals/metal products/ engineering	1,203	9,671	+8,468	+703
Other manufacture	544	619	+75	+14
Electricity, gas and water	720	1,451	+731	+102
Building and construction	5,426	6,817	+1,391	+26
Commerce (wholesale/retail)	11,378	13,182	+1,804	+16
Insurance/finance/business services	808	2,773	+1,965	+243
Transport/communication/ storage	4,124	5,707	+1,583	+38
Public administration/defence	2,952	4,956	+2,004	+68
Professional services	6,955	13,928	+6,973	+100
Personal services	5,117	4,726	−391	−8
Other industries	923	1,269	+346	+37
Total	94,112	97,470	+3,358	+4

FIGURE 38

EMPLOYMENT IN THE ADJACENT REGIONS TO THE MID WEST
(CORK/KERRY AND GALWAY/MAYO), 1961–1986[3]

Industrial group	1961	1986	Change	% Change
Agriculture/forestry/fishing	129,943	56,518	−73,425	−57
Mining/extractive	1,294	1,311	+17	0
Manufacturing				
Food	8,444	9,925	+1,481	+17
Beverage/tobacco	1,432	1,443	+11	0
Textiles/clothing/footwear/ leather	10,070	6,618	−3,452	−34
Wood/wood products	2,024	3,449	+1,425	+70
Paper and printing	1,513	1,907	+394	+26
Chemicals/rubber/plastic products	3,339	4,956	+1,617	+48
Glass/pottery/cement	797	1,899	+1,102	+38
Metals/metal products/ engineering	2,957	13,955	+10,998	+372
Other manufacture	2,430	1,775	−655	−26
Electricity, gas and water	1,876	2,931	+1,055	+56
Building and construction	14,148	18,155	+4,007	+28
Commerce (wholesale/retail)	31,347	36,178	−307,295	+15
Insurance/finance/business services	2,478	6,910	+4,432	+179
Transport/communication/ storage	10,550	11,880	+1,330	+13
Public administration/defence	7,035	12,048	−68,303	+71
Professional services	20,096	40,037	+19,941	+99
Personal services	13,351	13,815	+464	+3
Other industries	1,855	3,138	+1,283	+69
Total	266,979	248,848	+18,131	+7

Electricity can be discounted as outside SFADCo's influence (it was due to specific investments by the Electricity Supply Board). The faster expansion of the two manufacturing groups can be attributed to the presence of SFADCo. Similarly, growth in the transport sector was related to Shannon Airport and the transport aspects of tourism, also affected by SFADCo policies. The faster Mid West growth in 'insurance/finance/business services' is significant. It would have been influenced by SFADCo in a number of ways, such as international office operations and spin-offs from high growth in metals and electronics.

These four 'high' growth sectors can therefore be examined in terms of how much of the growth is attributable to national measures and how much to regional measures. Presumably, if SFADCo had never existed, it would be reasonable to expect that the four sectors would have grown at the same percentage rate as the adjacent regions (i.e. the 'expected' rate as shown in Figure 39). But the actual rate was higher than this. Thus the difference between the actual and expected rates can be explained by the existence in the Mid West of a regional measure, giving an indication of the specific effect of SFADCo as distinct from the national measures which it or other agencies were applying.

Comparing the growth in employment of what *actually* happened against what *would* have happened had the Mid West experienced similar growth rates as the adjacent regions, shows a difference of over 7,300 jobs spread for the four sectors over the period.

The conclusion from this is that regionally-based programmes can be instrumental in generating significant extra employment growth above and beyond that achieved by national measures. This growth is spread over a number of manufacturing and service sectors. It may also be true to say that the difference is more discernible over a wider time span, and may not be so evident over short time scales.

A counter argument to this conclusion is represented by the 'displacement effect', the extent to which SFADCo diverted developments from adjacent regions to the Mid West. The amount of such a displacement would need to be subtracted from difference between the Mid West and the others to give a fuller evaluation of SFADCo.

FIGURE 39

ACTUAL AND EXPECTED EMPLOYMENT CHANGE (MAIN GROWTH SECTORS)
IN THE MID WEST REGION, 1961–86

Sector	Actual	Expected	Difference
Chemical, rubber, plastic products	+1,977	+202	+1,775
Metals, metal products, machinery	+8,468	+4,475	+3,993
Insurance, finance, business services	+1,965	+1,446	+519
Transport/comunication/storage	+1,583	+536	+1,047
Total	+13,993	+6,659	+7,334

III

Conclusions

THIRTEEN

Towards the Third Paradigm – Leaders, Visions and Networks

THIS CHAPTER attempts to reach some conclusions on the implications of the SFADCo case study for the field of knowledge known as local and regional development. We return to the challenge posed by James Grant.

> The intervention of governments to help under-developed or dis-tressed areas is generally based on ideology, or political pressure, or on someone's hunch. We need a much more scientific approach to these matters, based on practical experience in the field.[1]

This study thus attempts to emulate the 'scientific' or data gathering approach.

We can conclude by reviewing the use of the two paradigms of regional development – development from above and development from below. Both paradigms are found to have validity, but conversely neither offers an adequate framework for explaining the SFADCo experience. Certainly the role of central institutions, national government and inward investment was crucial, pointing to 'development from above' principles. However, community relationships, local activism and indigenous enterprise were also central features, confirming aspects of 'development from below'. The study thus shows that neither of the two paradigms is effective in evalu-ating the story.

Consequently, we need to commence a search towards a third paradigm, one that embraces appropriate elements of the previous two. The third paradigm should focus more clearly on the uncertainties and irregularities in development, rather than imposing some sort of patterned order as the previous two attempted. Thus the third paradigm could be distinguished from the previous two by its greater acceptance of the discontinuities inherent in regional development. See Figure 40.

167

FIGURE 40

CHARACTERISTICS OF OLD AND NEW PARADIGMS

Old Paradigms	New Paradigm
Plans	Discontinuities
Science	Irregularities
Patterns	Coincidences
Continuities	Intuition
Regularities	Absence of pattern

The new paradigm needs to be created through a series of building blocks, each providing a different element. These building blocks can be identified through practical research in development experience and this study highlights three such building blocks. They can be seen as elements playing a role in successful development programmes. Where these elements are present, and closely interrelated and mutually supportive, then the resultant development programmes could be potentially strengthened. But where these elements are not present, or are not adequately integrated with each other, then development programmes based on them could face possible weaknesses.

The three elements are leadership, vision and networks. *Leadership* implies motivation, influence, originality, problem-solving and confidence: this could be generated by an individual or group. *Vision* is about global aims, goals, ideals, dreams, sense of mission and values. *Networks* are represented by contacts between people, loyalties, support groups, informal associations, unofficial collaboration and personal coalitions. The argument here is that successful development can be bolstered by leadership and powered by vision embedded within a supporting network of personal contacts. The mutually reinforcing interaction between leadership, vision and networks can potentially strengthen all three. Leadership can provide the vision, but this vision must be shared and developed through networks of personal contacts.

These three factors suggest some building blocks for the third paradigm, but do not exclude others that could be illuminated from research into additional case studies.

LEADERSHIP

The issue of leadership has attracted a considerable literature. This has suggested a range of diverse definitions of the concept. One definition has been suggested as follows:

Leadership is an influence relationship among leaders and followers who intend real changes that reflect their mutual purposes.[2]

The topic of leadership thus contains a series of related themes:

- Influence: Emphasis on persuasion, prestige, personality, inter-personal skills, rational discussion, reputation, non-coercive relationships.
- Leaders/followers: A two-way relationship between leaders and followers; followers actively participate in the leadership relationship; the relationship is unequal; however, followers are not passive, they are positive participants.
- Change: There is a purposeful direction to change and something is being transformed, agreed by leaders and followers; there is a joint intention that binds them together for tangible changes.
- Mutual purpose: Aims and goals are held in common by a community of believers.

Leadership must be distinguished from management and administration. Leadership goes beyond the latter two. It is concerned with the setting of goals and missions, and in creating a social organism around those aims. Leadership is specifically focused on the 'ends' of endeavour, rather than the 'means' which capture the attention of managers and administrators. Leadership transforms a formal organisation into a social institution, infused with character, purpose and goals. Leadership is value-driven, concerned with change, construction and creativity: it is not neutral or technical.[3]

The literature on leadership follows a series of diverse paths, many of them contradictory and divergent. Figure 41 summarises the theories of leadership.

Early research on leadership tended to focus on the personal make-up, social background, characteristics and traits of leaders, with individual personality seen as intrinsic to leadership. It attempted to identify the attributes of prominent leaders that set them apart from others, the assumption being that knowledge of such traits could be used to predict future leaders.[4]

An alternative approach was to focus on the behaviour of leaders rather than their characteristics i.e. what a person does rather than what a person is. This tradition of research sought to identify patterns or style of leadership, and the relationship between leadership style and organisational effectiveness. Debates here were about the most appropriate style of leadership: authoritarian or collaborative; task-oriented or group-oriented.

FIGURE 41

THEORIES OF LEADERSHIP

Theory	Emphasis
The 'positive' view:	Leadership contributes to development, and flows from diverse factors
Personality	Characteristics and traits of leader
Behaviour	Style of leader
Contingency	Interaction between leader and environment
Situation	Leadership dependent on social context
The 'negative' view:	Leadership has negative role in development
Inequality	Leadership creates dependence
'Halo effect'	Leadership is romanticised
Middle ground:	Leadership acts in wider context
Systems view	Interactions between leadership, policy and administration

The assumption was that such leadership styles could be acquired through training.[5]

The 'contingency' approach occupies a middle ground between the first two theories. It argues that no single 'best' leadership style exists: the most effective leaders adapt their behaviour to their surroundings and to the task in hand. Leadership is dependent on the interaction between leader and environment. Emergence of leadership is dependent on the contingencies of a particular context – type of group, organisation and task.[6]

In contrast to the first three theories, a 'situationist' school of thought sees leadership as dependent on the situation from which it arises, a situation rooted in the surrounding organisational context or cultural values. Patterns of leadership are grounded in the institutions of society – roles, expectations, norms and prevailing attitudes. Leadership arises to fit the surrounding social environment.[7]

These four sets of assumptions tended to view leadership in a positive light. The debate was about the diverse factors contributing to effective leadership, and how successful leadership could be achieved. In opposition to this, a contrasting set of assumptions was to question, or challenge, the role of leadership, representing the view that leadership made a restricted, or indeed negative, contribution to development.

One particular view is that leadership exacerbates the development problem. Leadership derives from a relationship of inequality and depresses rather than promotes initiative. Leadership roles are frequently taken by those already endowed with advantage, thus reinforcing pre-existing structures of inequality. Existing power holders become more powerful. Reliance on leadership weakens development: it cements inequality and promotes dependence.[8]

A softer but still negative view is that the contribution of leadership is exaggerated, part of a 'halo effect'. People like to attribute performance to an individual rather than a group. This attribution, although mistaken, can be functional: it personalises the organisation and promotes motivation. Participants tend to romanticise the role of a leader, making it part of myth and legend. The leadership factor is often used to explain success or failure, in spite of the realities of the situation which may be clearly otherwise. The 'team manager' syndrome attributes winning or losing personally to an individual manager, irrespective of other factors. But such explanations, it is argued, reflect the bias of the observers and not the true picture.[9]

As middle ground between the positive and negative theories of leadership, the 'systems' approach sees leadership as a factor of limited importance, but still playing a role. The argument has been put that leadership alone plays a restricted role in development. There is a 'three legged stool' of policy, organisation and leadership. The issue is not the relative importance of each, but rather to recognise the interaction and complementarity of the three elements. Effective development requires the integration of the three.[10]

Lessons from the SFADCo case study

These considerations thus highlight the different and contradictory views of leadership and the role of leadership in the development process. Turning back to SFADCo, it is appropriate to examine the insights provided by the case study for these debates. The question arising from the SFADCo case study is the extent to which, if at all, leadership can play a positive role in development and, if so, what sort of role that might be. Certainly, a continuous feature emanating out of the SFADCo experience was the issue of leadership. Brendan O'Regan's qualities as a leader were cited time after time, particularly his enchanting ability to influence people:

> Brendan O'Regan was the supreme influencer of people . . . using
> them in a sense, but in the most positive way.[11]

That was how Jack Lynch (one of the SFADCo management team) put it. O'Regan's leadership emerges as a dominant force in the history of Shannon – establishing the early Sales and Catering organisation, building up a sound management team, coordinating the search for a new form of development at Shannon, calling public meetings, putting together the different parts. His influence on key decision-making and investors was powerful and dramatic. The SFADCo files are replete with notes of personal meetings and 'Dear Brendan' letters from people like Erskine Childers, senior civil servants, Lord Gort, John Hunt, the Andrews family and many others. What is clear from these files, and the stories associated with them, is that Brendan O'Regan effectively used his very charming personality as a tool to gain allegiance and win support. He drew people to him, spurred them on and inspired them with his dreams.

The leadership of Brendan O'Regan was most pronounced in the early days of SFADCo – 1959–67 – producing a clear vision of what was needed i.e. a focus on the airport, with constant brainstorming and intensive teamwork. He exerted a remarkable personal influence and charisma on those about him, one that extended to other entrepreneurs, activists and investors such as hoteliers, industrialists, business leaders and politicians. His was an immense personal magnetism that motivated and drove others.

However, for his subsequent years as chairman (1967–77) and his later years as a board member (1977–85), Brendan O'Regan's objectives gradually changed and developed. In 1967, the remit of SFADCo was extended to a wider range of regional development functions, covering a broader geographic area. This coincided with an extension of the O'Regan vision to other issues and he became heavily involved in a series of new ventures, some distance removed not only from Shannon Airport but also from the specifics of regional industrial development.

Brendan O'Regan's interest during the late 1960s and 1970s spread over a number of innovative measures: he initiated studies on organisational aspects of Gaeltacht development (Irish-speaking areas on the Western seaboard); he encouraged a new unit to promote overseas development aid to Third World countries by SFADCo and was instrumental in the establishment of a state-sponsored body (Devco) to do this nationally; he worked intensively in the formation of Rent an Irish Cottage and a related Buy an Irish Cottage scheme; he pushed for the idea of a World Trade Centre at Shannon. In 1977, Brendan O'Regan established, with others, Cooperation North, a non-political association aiming to draw the two communities in the island of Ireland closer together, and he subsequently worked with great commitment to build it up and secure its financing. He also set up the Irish Peace Institute.

Because of these involvements, Brendan O'Regan's vision began to progressively distance itself from others in SFADCo. He became more remote from its ongoing regional industrial and airport traffic promotion. The management team under Paul Quigley was pursuing strong priorities with limited resources. O'Regan sought to steer the agency into areas of special interest to himself, particularly those relating to village development and Cooperation North; Quigley saw these as diversions from the company's given tasks in which success would be measured by jobs created and by airport traffic flows. Quigley's was not a narrow vision; it included matters ranging from urban redevelopment at the regional centre to promoting third level education. But the differences were great, and the result was disagreement and tension between the two men.

It was a measure of O'Regan's dominant personality and ability to sell ideas that the SFADCo board accepted his 1977 proposal to change its remit from the government which would take the company out of industrial development and into things closer to his interests. But it was a vindication of the executive's realism that Minister O'Malley rejected these proposals, giving the company a new and stronger industrial remit.

Two general points can be made about the story of leadership in SFADCo. The first point is that the experience does highlight the issue of individual personality and leadership in development. We will look more closely at this point now.

Role of leadership

O'Regan's style comes very close to that of the charismatic leader in the sociology literature. The concept of charismatic leader was first coined by the German sociologist Max Weber in the last century.[12] Max Weber highlighted how a leader's authority could be derived from charisma and attract allegiance by virtue of his unique attributes and abilities, exemplary qualities of an individual personality. According to Weber, charismatic leaders seize the task for which they are destined and attract others to follow them by virtue of their mission. Subsequent research in the twentieth century has highlighted the role of charismatic leaders in religious and political movements, and also in business organisations. It is in periods of rapid social change, or political upheaval, that charismatic leaders are most likely to appear.

The example of Brendan O'Regan would suggest that charismatic leadership has a potential role to play in development. Charismatic leaders have the ability to overturn traditional structures and ride rough-shod over bureaucratic procedures. O'Regan was very good at that. For localities in change, seeking new development goals and objectives, charismatic leaders can be significant in constructing these goals and visions and in motivating other people to work to them. O'Regan was good at that too. Charismatic leaders can potentially draw together diverse pressure groups in the development process, help them overcome their differences and establish a unified energy in one agreed direction. The O'Regan team brought together trade unions and others to secure local agreement.

The general conclusion here would be that charismatic leaders could have three possible functions for development:

- Replace traditional or bureaucratic procedures with new programmes more appropriate to emerging conditions.
- Establish new goals and win their acceptance.
- Provide a focal point to unify different economic pressure groups and interest groups.

The factor of charismatic leadership thus emerges as a significant feature in development. Charisma is thus potentially a very powerful force. But it also has its limitations. Charismatic leaders must cope with the frustrations of organisational life. In particular, charismatic vision may be remote from the operational realities. Bryman argues that there are some disadvantages with charismatic leadership in business settings.[13] He claims that charismatic leaders are inclined to be obsessive about their vision and use their persuasive powers to get others behind their dreams. The key, according to Bryman, is to ensure some control but without stifling initiative and creativity.

Max Weber had seen this dilemma one hundred years earlier. This was the issue called 'routinisation'. As the charismatic leader's dreams became fulfilled into reality, a new type of leadership emerged, one that based its authority on legal and rational grounds, rather than the original charisma, and was more concerned with operational issues. Inevitably the relationship between the two impulses – charismatic and operational – must be managed.

How was this balance achieved in the SFADCo leadership? This author has the impression that a strong and positive balance was struck throughout the development of Shannon during the 1960s. The initiation of the industrial estate, new town and tourist developments was spurred by a strong sense of mission, crusading zeal, purpose and moral spirit, all matched by an equally strong measure of pragmatism and realism. But this balance between the two approaches seems to have weakened during the 1970s, reflected by the difference of opinion on company policy between Brendan O'Regan and Paul Quigley's management team. This debate within SFADCo in the 1970s suggests some echoes of the possible tension between the charismatic leaders and their associates. It indicates that, while charismatic leadership is a potential ingredient, it needs to be integrated and balanced with other forces in the organisation. Once this balance is weakened, the resultant tension can hamper or undermine development programmes. But if the balance is maintained, the resultant energies can produce significant results.

Environment of policy and administration

The second general point about leadership in development is to show that it is only important in the context of a supportive environment. This is echoed in a comment by Paul Quigley:

> The key SFADCo lesson is that quite different management approaches can work in regional development, provided these approaches are competent and adequately empowered and funded.[14]

Paul Quigley's comment strongly reflects the systems view of leadership. The process of leadership is seen as one element in a wider canvas, the critical issue being the context of policy and administration and how that context provides a framework for leadership in development. Certainly there is evidence that the policy and administrative environments provided a very conducive atmosphere. Leadership emerged as a team effort involving several organisations and individuals spurred by policy and administrative supports.

The first of these other elements – policy support – was definitely present in substantial measure. National policies represented a critical framework for such leadership, providing the initiative for much of what happened at Shannon. The SFADCo operation can be seen as the implementation of a series of economic policies devised by the government. The Department of Finance study on Economic Development and the First Programme for Economic Expansion in the late 1950s created the policy impetus for SFADCo's creation. The Second Programme for Economic Expansion in the early 1960s set ambitious targets for national growth. The Third Programme in the late 1960s drew up challenging goals for full employment. Many of the objectives of these plans were not realised but they did bestow important psychological benefits and imbued the official bodies concerned with a strong sense of urgency and priority.

SFADCo was very much an outcome of those policies. The development of the initial industrial estate was marked by supportive legislation and generous incentives. Funding to SFADCo was considerable, amounting in 1970 to over 20% of Ireland's public capital programme for industry. The agency attracted the personal support and enthusiasm of the Taoiseach and senior members of government.

In terms of administration, the second dimension, there were significant measures on which SFADCo could draw. During the 1960s there was a marked government emphasis on providing relative discretion and independence to state-sponsored bodies i.e. agencies under public ownership but outside the mainstream civil service. A number of such organisations were established in the 1950s and 1960s in the industrial, trade and services sectors, enjoying significant support from central government with considerable autonomy and freedom of decision-making.

SFADCo was one such organisation. As an administrative entity it was endowed with a number of strengths. The board membership included both civil servants and local activists, bringing both sides together. In this structure, links to both national organisations and local interests were intensive and effective. Also, the legal framework of a limited company combined the twin benefits of freedom of action and public accountability. SFADCo had extensive legal powers and wide terms of reference within the context of public control.

Consequently, the two dimensions of policy and administration provided a vital framework within which local teamwork and leadership could be secured and enacted.

Returning to the general leadership issue, we can bring together the two strands of leadership personality and policy/administration factors. The concluding observation could be to suggest that personal leadership can play a critical role in the incipient stages of development programmes. It is at the phase of start-up or strategic change that leadership matters most: the situation is relatively unstructured, uncertainty is considerable and objectives are potentially in conflict. The function of leadership to define goals and missions is at its most critical here. However, such leadership can only be acted out within an environment of policy and administration and any leadership is an integral part of that context. Furthermore, leadership is part of the life-cycle of an organisation. As development programmes grow and mature, the issue of personal leadership reduces in significance and merges into the background of organisational structure and policy definition.

VISION

Goals are central to organisations as they represent a desired future state of affairs which the organisation seeks to realise. Goals serve many functions, such as:

- Orientation for the organisation.
- Guidelines for activity.
- Source of justification and legitimation for the organisation.
- Measuring rods to assess effectiveness and efficiency.

Goals of organisations are set in a number of ways – sometimes formally through a vote of members, or through a process of consultation and dialogue involving insiders and outsiders, or through a power-play between several pressure groups. Individual personalities and informal relationships also play a critical role in goal formation.[15]

Within the context of goals and their purposes, the concept of vision has been mentioned. A vision is a construct of the future that generates excitement and vitality[16] – one type of goal. It is distinguished from other categories of goals in that it specifically appeals to emotions, values, loyalty and feelings. Visions are goals with strong motivational powers.

The literature on leadership is heavily imbued with the theme of vision. Ability to 'envision' a future, devise a mental image of what might be achieved or construct a set of values around this image and communicate it to others is a central part of the development process. The story of SFADCo is itself a very good case study of the role of vision in development, Paul Quigley highlighting this in a 1987 conference paper:

> An absolute truth about human nature, and one too often neglected, is simply this: that the more clearly and vividly we describe and visualise an aim, the more likely we are to achieve it. That truth was evident to the caveman who made paintings of his quarry on the walls of his home ... if bringing about the future situation will need effort and commitment, then surely the description of that must be such as to speak to people's hearts as well as to their heads.[17]

The purpose of vision in motivation has been highlighted by a number of authors. The clarification of common goals is critical to the exercise of power and authority and human beings resent being left in the dark about the ends of an enterprise in which they are engaged.[18] The simple act of affirming a common goal is frequently enough in itself to release human energies to an astounding extent. Vision in leadership is a critical factor in motivating behaviour. Vision needs to be developed in a number of ways:

- Clearly expressed.
- Well explained to others.
- Extended to real life situations.
- Expanded to cover new circumstances.

Vision must also satisfy two other conditions – it must have some solid content and substance and it must be realised in practical steps. Without this solid substance and achievement vision quickly degenerates into frothy nothingness.[19]

The construction and use of a vision is an interaction of several elements. Firstly, a vision must be created and crafted – vision must be designed, so to speak. Secondly, vision needs to be represented to other people – it has to be communicated, transmitted, given vitality. Thirdly, vision demands an active audience to participate in it, assist in it and transform it further. Thus vision has almost a quality of drama about it with script, actors and audience.[20]

The mechanics of enacting vision have to be effective. Vision has to be transformed from a personal dream, held by a few, into a social goal, shared by many. Enacting vision into acceptance and reality involves extensive skills in leadership and human relations.[21]

The SFADCo experience

Throughout the early history of SFADCo, and also into subsequent years, vision building played a very prominent role as an element in the development process. The first phases of Shannon were intimately bound up with a sense of nationalistic pride. Brendan O'Regan put it thus: 'The driving force was patriotism. We wanted to prove that the Irish were as good as any others on the international scene.'[22]

A critical vehicle for transmitting the vision, and debating it with others, were the public meetings at Shannon. These succeeded in the development of a shared and collective goal for local people. The vision had also to be communicated commercially too. O'Regan explained that he and his people were involved in major public relations to convince the airlines that if they abandoned Shannon they were losing a 'potential market'. Thus the vision had to be promoted to different audiences, both at home and overseas. Brendan O'Regan commented: 'We had to talk people into believing the vision.'[23]

But the vision was not restricted to Shannon. There was vision in the air and the whole country was imbued with it. Tom Callanan put it this way:

> It was a very exciting time. The country was shaking off its lethargy and the psychological damage done by the massive emigration of the previous decade. There was enormous support from people like Lemass, Whitaker, C.H. Murray and others. There was almost unprecedented enthusiasm for development . . . the atmosphere was right.[24]

Peter Donnelly too emphasised this. He remarked: 'the tremendous excitement, everybody talking about development, everybody keyed up, they knew what they had to do, if not how to go about it.'[25]

The strength of the vision, and the powerful impulses it generated, comes across in all these statements. But it is also true that vision must be reinforced by reality, the early Dáil debates being a case in point. Initially there was much scepticism, but this later gave way to enthusiasm. However, what did this was not the quality of the vision but the results. As employment began to grow at Shannon, the vision came to be justified. Acceptance and support grew as concrete and tangible benefits emerged. This indicates that vision, if it is to survive, needs some practical outcome.

This overview of vision in SFADCo suggests a number of conclusions about vision in development.

- It illustrates graphically how collective shared vision wins support and motivates people. Debate, discussion and communications are building blocks for vision. Through vision allies can be won and support galvanised. The content of the vision is critical – clear image, crisp objective, coherent logic, appealing to both emotion and reason.
- But vision needs a solid base. Without some short-term results it can become meaningless. Vision alone is not enough and achievement must follow.
- The vision needs to be related to the external political and social environment, and must be consistent with it. The environment must be supportive of the vision, giving it life.

But overarching all this is the necessity for vision to be shared and communicated through a series of channels i.e. the contact networks of the people involved. To this issue we now turn.

NETWORKS

The history of Shannon is typified by alliances, allegiances and supportive networks. The SFADCo leadership drew heavily on personal contacts – O'Regan's links with Sean Lemass and his departmental secretary John Leydon, other contacts with decision makers and connections with local interest groups and operators all eased and smoothed their path.

This experience illustrates the role in local development played by contact networks. Such networks have been defined in terms of people or groups involved in long-term relationships. Networks thus comprise two components: positions in the networks (represented by the roles of the participants) and the links between them (representing the relationships). The argument is that resources flow between these points along these links, aiding the participants.[26]

The positive role of contact networks in development has an emerging and substantial literature. The term regional innovation complex has been coined to show how innovation emerges from the synergy of local inter-action between participants in the public, private and educational sectors. This has been illustrated by research in Spain, Italy and Japan.[27] In Austria, local cooperation by network had a significant effect in regenerating declining industrial areas.[28] Studies of rural Missouri in the USA have shown that local leaders are typified as having strong personal connections with both external official organisations and local groups.[29] Social networks gave competitive advantage to business entrepreneurs in Washington State.[30]

Networks serve a number of functions for development, represented by the range of different resources that flow between the participants:

- Finance and monetary assets.
- Ideas and innovations.
- Information.
- Values and moral support.

Thus participants may draw a number of assets from networks ranging from finance to the sharing of ideas and information, including moral support and encouragement from other members of the network.

Networks have been classified as being of several types and can be categorised according to a number of criteria:

FIGURE 42

ALTERNATIVE CLASSIFICATIONS OF CONTACT NETWORKS

Formal (written rules and procedures)	or	informal (personal networks)
Large (many members)	or	small (few members)
Related (many inter-connections)	or	non-related (few inter-connections)
Tight (intensive contact)	or	loose (intermittent contact)

Contact networks between people or groups are likely to be multifaceted and will contain elements of many of these characteristics, thus falling between the two extremes. There are therefore few 'pure' contact networks of one single category.

A significant amount of research has been undertaken into the role of networks in economic development and some key conclusions can be summarised as follows:

- Networks support local and regional development through access to resources: finance, information, moral support.

- The most effective networks are large and loose, involving participants in a very wide range of contacts, providing access to the most extensive range of information and ideas. Contrasting networks that are small and tight are less versatile: they potentially constrict fresh thinking by the members and are less open to new ideas.[31]

- Networks fulfil different functions at different stages of the development of a project. At the initial entrepreneurial phase, networks provide access to information and ideas. The social or informal network is critical here. As projects develop, networks become more formalised and focused, emphasising organisational linkages.[32]

- The informal element of networks is always significant, represented by power, influence, trust and friendship networks.[33]

- Different types of innovators use networks in different ways. Community activists, promoting public or non-commercial projects, exploit large and diffuse networks. However, business and commercial innovators are more restricted in their range of network, probably due to the exigencies of commercial confidentiality.[34]

SFADCo and networks

It is thus useful to examine the experience of SFADCo in terms of what it can teach about the role of networks in development.

Contact networks loomed large as tools used by Brendan O'Regan and his SFADCo team. O'Regan's initial connections with holders of power were through the Stephen's Green Club in Dublin where he caught the attention of Sean Lemass and John Leydon. As Shannon began to develop, this network of influential contacts widened still further – Tod Andrews (CIE), Tim O'Driscoll (Bord Fáilte), Jerry Dempsey (Aer Lingus) and J.P. Beddy (IDA) – providing active encouragement for the Shannon project. The point is that the support from these people was influenced by their personal connections with O'Regan as well as any formal evaluation of the project. Thus mutual trust, confidence, loyalties and personal ties were the building blocks for the network. The commitment of the individual decision-makers soon found its way down the ranks of their respective organisations. Tom Callanan explained: 'The executives down the line knew the bosses wanted solutions, so solutions were found.'[35]

But as well as spreading upward through the power structure of Dublin, the networks also extended locally to business, trade unions, political representatives, service providers and local authorities. Networks of personal contacts were vital ingredients in overcoming obstacles, winning support and securing acceptance. This comes across particularly clearly in the early years of the industrial estate where intensive local collaboration needed to be secured with trade unions, transport operators, customs officials and others. Without the lubricating influence of personal contacts, much of this cooperation could have stalled through procedural friction. The network spread internationally too. Individual investors such as the Andrews family (Knappogue) and others both in the tourism, industry and transport sectors were also involved.

On a general level, the SFADCo experience provides examples of several aspects of networks:

- Personal contacts were most significant in the earliest days of the venture. At that time, there were few procedures or formal guidelines by which the development could be implemented. As the project grew in implementation, formal procedures grew in relative significance. So the SFADCo history confirms the role of informal contacts in project formation.
- Thus the informal dimension played a critical role in these early networks. But the informality or personal dimension should not be over-emphasised. Paul Quigley commented: 'These connections represented good relationships. But they were not personal friendships. They were contacts based on knowledge and respect.'[36]

- The case study would suggest that the informal element plays a role but only in the wider context of formal structures. Hence the key issue is the relationship between the informal and formal aspects, and how informal roles are played out within the setting of official structures.
- The SFADCo network can be described as having a number of characteristics:
  1. a mixture of informal and formal elements;
  2. large, involving local, national and international participants;
  3. non-related in that participants came from diverse origins and were not heavily inter-connected, apart from their common SFADCo link;
  4. loose in that contact was relatively intermittent rather than frequent.

Hence the SFADCo example illustrates a comparatively open, heterogeneous and diffused network, involving different people from contrasting backgrounds. It stands at the opposite extreme to the small, close-knit or homogeneous network of similar people. The SFADCo case study demonstrates the value of heterogeneous networks, providing a wide spread of ideas, information and perceptions. The range of options and opportunities generated by such a network would have been more extensive than that allowed by a narrow group of similar-minded people. It was this heterogeneity of network that forged a peculiar strength of the SFADCo development.

CONCLUDING COMMENT

The case study demonstrates that the two established paradigms of development from above and development from below are both deficient in failing to provide an effective framework for interpreting SFADCo. A third paradigm is needed that reflects the uncertainties and coincidences of development processes such as this. The third paradigm should be constructed with building blocks arising out of practical experience in the field of regional development and embrace elements of the former two. Three such building blocks are suggested as arising from this particular study and deserving particular attention:

- Personal leadership within a supportive environment of policy and administration.
- Visions that define a desired future state of affairs in an exciting manner.

- Networks of personal contacts, diffused over diverse groups and categories of people.

On the level of methodology, this exercise demonstrates the validity of the case-study method in development and organisational studies i.e. archival investigation and personal interviews set within a context of literature and previous research. The approach has been shown to generate useful information, rich in content and insight.

Endnotes

INTRODUCTION

1 Hetherington, 1990
2 Yin, 1989

CHAPTER ONE

1 Turpin, 1991
2 Bennett, 1989
3 Valesco, 1991
4 Tierney, 1984
5 Eurada, 1993
6 International Labour Office, 1944
7 Ibid.
8 Jones, 1983
9 Neuse, 1983
10 Hargrove and Conkin, 1984
11 Neuse, 1983
12 Gwin, 1987
13 Chandler, 1984
14 Selznick, 1966
15 Hansen, 1974
16 Santaniello, 1983
17 Podbielski, 1978
18 Bachtler and Michie, 1989
19 Podbielski, 1978
20 Ibid.
21 Fried, 1974
22 Grant, 1990
23 Grassie, 1983
24 Hetherington, 1990
25 Grant, 1990
26 Quoted in Grassie, 1983

27 Micks, 1925
28 Ibid.
29 Ibid.
30 Lee, 1989
31 Aalen, Whelan and Stout, 1997

CHAPTER TWO

1 Friedmann and Alonso, 1964
2 McKee, Dean and Leahy, 1970
3 Friedmann, 1966
4 Ibid.
5 Perroux, 1955
6 Hirschmann, 1958
7 Myrdal, 1957
8 Seers, 1977
9 Stohr and Taylor, 1981
10 Sanyal, 1994
11 Stohr in Albrechts, 1989

CHAPTER THREE

1 Nystrom and Starbuck, 1981
2 Hodgets, 1991
3 Bass, 1990
4 Etzioni, 1964
5 Blau and Scott, 1963
6 Seers, 1977
7 Stohr, 1989
8 Friedmann, 1966
9 Seers, 1977
10 Stohr and Taylor, 1981
11 Coombes, 1989

CHAPTER FOUR

1 Information for the case study is drawn from three sources: published material, personal interviews and documentation from company archives. Published material and interviews are noted as sources where appropriate. In all other cases, the information has been derived from archives.
2 Department of Finance, 1958
3 Foster, 1988
4 Interview with Brendan O'Regan
5 Ibid.
6 Interview with Jack Lynch
7 Dáil debates, 28 January 1947
8 Interview with Jack Lynch
9 Interview with Peter Donnelly
10 Internal memorandum, 1955
11 Interview with Peter Donnelly
12 *Proposals for Industrial and Commercial Development at Shannon* by Urwick Orr Consultants, 1957
13 The work was divided into these categories in 'divisions' and allocated to Sales and Catering executives: Jack Lynch, Jack Ryan, Joe McElgunn and Peter Donnelly, with O'Regan as 'chief executive'. In addition, a 'consultative committee' was established to provide discussion and advice, comprising R.C. O'Connor (Department of Industry and Commerce), Col. P. Maher (Airport Manager, Department of Industry and Commerce), J. Buist MacKenzie (Urwick Orr Consultants) and Brendan O'Regan.
14 Interview with Peter Donnelly
15 Interview with Jack Lynch
16 Interview with Peter Donnelly
17 Ibid.
18 Ibid.
19 Report of Shannon Free Airport Development Authority, 1958

20 Memorandum to Government, December 1958
21 The first board members of SFADCO were: R.C. O'Connor (Department of Industry and Commerce) J.Buist MacKenzie (Urwick Orr Consultants), Col. P. Maher (Airport Manager, Department of Industry and Commerce), J.J. Walsh (Industrial Development Authority), A. Kennan (Department of Industry and Commerce), G. Farren (Irish Steel), N. Huggard (hotelier), Brendan O'Regan (chairman).
22 Interview with Peter Donnelly
23 Note of meeting in Shannon, February 1959
24 Dáil debates, 21 October 1959
25 Letter to Brendan O'Regan from Erskine Childers, 1959
26 Correspondence with the author

CHAPTER FIVE

1 SFADCo files
2 Interview with Brendan O'Regan
3 Ibid.
4 Internal memorandum, 1971
5 Interview with Brendan O'Regan
6 Ibid.
7 Ibid.
8 Interview with Paul Quigley
9 Interview with Peter Donnelly
10 Letter to Brendan O'Regan from Erskine Childers, 1965
11 Note of a meeting in Shannon, 1968
12 SFADCo press statement, 1968
13 RIC files, 1973
14 RIC files, 1972
15 Interview with Paul Quigley
16 Interview with Peter Donnelly
17 Interview with Paul Quigley
18 Interview with Peter Donnelly
19 Ibid.

20 Friedmann, 1989
21 Letter from Erskine Childers, 1959
22 SFADCo Annual Report, 1965
23 Letter from Erskine Childers to Brendan O'Regan, 1968
24 Letter to Department of Transport and Power from Paul Quigley, 1973
25 Interview with Peter Donnelly
26 Dáil debates, October 1959
27 Interview with Brendan O'Regan
28 Ibid.
29 Interview with Peter Donnelly
30 Nystrom and Starbuck, 1981
31 SFADCo files

CHAPTER SIX

1 Shannon Freeport brochure, March 1958
2 Dáil debates, 6 November 1958
3 Ibid.
4 Interview with Brendan O'Regan
5 Seanad debate, 18 November 1959
6 Interview with Tom Callanan
7 Interview with Peter Donnelly
8 Interview with Jack Lynch
9 Interview with Peter Donnelly
10 Dáil debates, 25 July 1961
11 Ibid.
12 Dáil debates, 19 July 1963 (Mr McQuillan)
13 Dáil debates, 9 May 1968
14 Ibid. (Mr P O'Donnell)
15 SFADCo files
16 Organisation for Economic Cooperation and Development (OECD), 1990
17 Interview with Tom Callanan
18 Ibid.
19 Ibid.
20 Ibid.
21 Porter, 1990
22 SFADCo annual reports
23 Mulcahy, 1985

24 Interview with Peter Donnelly
25 Interview with Tom Callanan
26 Collingridge, 1992
27 *Shannon Hinterland Survey* by E Vercruijsse, Leiden University, Netherlands, 1961
28 Conference paper by Paul Quigley, 1965
29 *Attitudes to Industrial Work at Shannon* by the Tavistock Institute, London, 1966
30 Interview with Peter Donnelly
31 Interview with Tom Callanan
32 SFADCo files
33 Ibid.
34 Ibid.
35 Ibid.
36 National Economic and Social Council, 1982
37 O'Malley, 1986
38 SFADCo files
39 Central Statistics Office

CHAPTER SEVEN

1 Interview with Peter Donnelly
2 Letter from Brendan O'Regan to Erskine Childers, April 1961
3 Dáil debates, 25 July 1961
4 Seanad debates, 3 August 1961
5 Correspondence with the Department of Transport and Power, 1961–62
6 *Preliminary Planning Proposals for Industrial and Community Development at Shannon* by Downes and Meehan Consultants, January 1962
7 *Report of the Inter-Departmental Committee on Housing at Shannon*, February 1962
8 Letter from Thekla Beere to Brendan O'Regan, January 1963
9 Dáil debates, 19 July 1963

10 Interview with Jack Lynch
11 Poulton, 1991
12 Interview with Paul Quigley
13 Interview with Jack Lynch
14 Ibid.
15 Interview with Paul Quigley
16 SFADCo annual report, 1970
17 White Paper on Local Government, 1974
18 White Paper on Industrial Policy, 1984
19 SFADCo files
20 Interview with Cian O'Carroll
21 Ryan, 1968
22 Interview with Jack Lynch
23 Ibid.
24 Interview with Cian O'Carroll

CHAPTER EIGHT

1 Buchanan, 1969
2 Interview with Tom Callanan
3 Irish Times, 24 October 1967
4 Seanad debates, 5 June 1968
5 Interview with Tom Callanan
6 Lichfield, 1967
7 Internal memorandum, 1968
8 Interview with Tom Callanan
9 Internal memorandum
10 Dáil debates, 4 July 1974
11 Interview with Tom Callanan
12 Regional Industrial Development, conference paper by Paul Quigley, 1973
13 Notes of Justin Keating's talk to SFADCo management, March 1977
14 Ibid.
15 Notes of Des O'Malley's meeting with SFADCo managment, August 1977
16 Interview with Paul Quigley
17 Interview with Des O'Malley
18 Ibid.
19 SFADCo annual report, 1975

CHAPTER NINE

1 Interview with Brendan O'Regan
2 Ibid.
3 Interview with Des O'Malley
4 Ibid.
5 Dáil debates, 31 January 1978
6 Tom O'Donnell, Dáil debates, 31 January 1978
7 Barry Desmond, Dáil debate, 31 January 1978
8 SFADCo files
9 Dáil debates, 15 October 1980
10 National Economic and Social Council, 1982
11 Pinchot, 1985
12 Dáil debates, 15 October 1980
13 Interview with Des O'Malley
14 Ibid.
15 Interview with Paul Quigley

CHAPTER TEN

1 Galbraith and Nathanson, 1978
2 Ibid.
3 Interview with Paul Quigley
4 Merton, 1957
5 SFADCo files
6 Ibid.
7 Interview with Peter Donnelly
8 Annual budget statements of the government

CHAPTER ELEVEN

1 Paper to the Institute of Engineers in Ireland by Paul Quigley, 1987
2 Posner, 1974
3 Paper to the Regional Studies Association by Paul Quigley, 1978
4 Ibid.
5 Ibid.
6 OECD, 1987

7   Barrington, 1980
8   Dáil debates, 21 October 1959
9   Interview with Fr Harry Bohan
10 Ibid.
11 Interview with Des O'Malley

CHAPTER TWELVE

1   Central Statistics Office
2   Ibid.
3   Ibid.

CHAPTER THIRTEEN

1   Grant, 1990
2   Rost, 1991
3   Selznick, 1957
4   Tucker, 1977
5   Tushman, 1989
6   Fiedler, 1981
7   Smith and Peterson, 1988
8   Friedmann, 1989
9   Meindl, 1985
10 Sawhill, 1989
11 Interview
12 Bryman, 1992

13 Ibid.
14 Interview with Paul Quigley
15 Etzioni, 1964
16 Sooklal, 1991
17 Paper by Paul Quigley to the
    Institute of Engineers in Ireland,
    Limerick, 1987
18 Lasswell, 1948
19 Sashkin, 1986
20 Westley and Mintzberg, 1989
21 Sooklal, 1991
22 Interview with Brendan O'Regan
23 Ibid.
24 Interview with Tom Callanan
25 Interview with Peter Donnelly
26 Thorelli, 1986
27 Stohr, 1986
28 Grabher, 1989
29 O'Brien, 1991
30 Butler and Hansen, 1991
31 Ibid.
32 Ibid.
33 Boissevain, 1974
34 Johannisson and Nilsson, 1989
35 Interview with Tom Callanan
36 Interview with Paul Quigley

Bibliography

Aalen, F., Whelan, K. and Stout, M. *Atlas of the Irish Rural Landscape* (Cork University Press, 1997)

Albrechts, L. *Regional Policy at the Crossroads* (Jessica Kingsley, London, 1989)

Alden, J. and Morgan, R. *Regional Planning – A Comprehensive View* (Leightan Buzzard, London, 1975)

Bachtler, J. and Michie, R. *European Regional Policy News* (Regional Studies Association, London, 1989)

Bass, B. *Handbook of Leadership* (Free Press, New York, 1990)

Barrington, T. *From Big Government to Local Government* (Institute of Public Administration, Dublin, 1980)

Bennett, R. *Territory and Administration in Europe* (Pinter, London, 1989)

Blau, P. and Scott, W. *Formal Organisations* (Routledge and Kegan Paul, London, 1963)

Boissevain, J. *Friends of Friends – Networks, Manipulators and Coalitions* (Blackwell, London, 1974)

Bryman, A. *Charisma and Leadership in Organisations* (Sage, London, 1992)

Buchanan, C. *Regional Development in Ireland* (An Foras Forbartha, Dublin, 1969)

Butler, J. and Hansen, G. *Network Evolution, Entrepreneurial Success and Regional Development* (Journal of Entrepreneurship and Regional Development, London, 1991)

Chandler, W. *The Myth of TVA* (Ballinger, New York, 1984)

Clout, H. *Regional Development in Western Europe* (David Fulton, London, 1987)

Collingridge, D. *The Management of Scale – Big Organisations, Big Decisions, Big Mistakes* (Routledge, London, 1992)

Coombes, D. *Economic Development Networks* (LEDA, Brussels, 1989)

Dáil Committee on Public Expenditure, *Review of Shannon Free Airport Development Company* (Dáil Eireann, Dublin, 1986)

Etzioni, A. *Modern Organisations* (Prentice Hall, New Jersey, 1964)

Eurada *Membership Directory of the European Association of Development Agencies* (Brussels, 1993)

191

Fiedler, F. *Leadership Effectiveness* (American Behavioural Scientist, New York, 1981)

Finance, Department of. *Economic Development* (Government Publications, Dublin, 1958)

Foster, R. *Modern Ireland* (Allen Lane, London, 1988)

Fried, R. 'Administrative Pluralism and Italian Regional Planning' in *Regional Policy* by Friedmann J. and Alonso, W. (MIT Press, Boston, 1974)

Friedmann, J. and Alonso, W. *Regional Development and Planning* (MIT Press, Boston, 1964)

Friedmann, J. *Regional Development Policy: A Case Study of Venezuela* (MIT Press, Boston, 1966)

Friedmann, J. *Empowerment: The Politics of Alternative Development* (Blackwell, Oxford, 1989)

Gage, R. and Mandell, M. *Strategies for Managing Intergovernmental Policies and Networks* (Praeger, New York, 1990)

Galbraith, J. and Nathanson, D. *Strategy Implementation: The Role of Structure and Process* (West Publishing, Minnesota, 1978)

Grabher, G. 'Regional Innovation by Networking: the Case of Southern Lower Austria' in *Journal of Entrepreneurship and Regional Development* (Taylor and Francis, London, 1989)

Grant, J. *A Long Term Assessment* in *Highlands and Islands – A Generation of Progress*, edited by A. Hetherington (Aberdeen University Press, Aberdeen, 1990)

Grassie, J. *Highland Experiment – The Story of the Highlands and Islands Development Board* (Aberdeen University Press, Aberdeen, 1983)

Gwin, L. 'Accountability at TVA: A Response' in *Forum for Applied Research and Public Policy* (University of Tennesse, New York, 1987)

Hansen, N. *Public Policy and Regional Economic Development* (MIT Press, Boston, 1974)

Hargrove, E. and Conkin, P. *TVA – Fifty Years of Grass Roots Bureaucracy* (University of Illinois Press, Chicago, 1984)

Hetherington, A. (ed.) *Highlands and Islands – A Generation of Progress* (Aberdeen University Press, Aberdeen, 1990)

Hirschmann, A. *The Strategy of Economic Development* (Yale University Press, New Haven, 1958)

Hodgets, R. *Organisational Behaviour – Theory and Practice* (Merrill, New York, 1991)

Hugh-Jones, E. 'The Tennessee Valley Authority Fifty Years On' in *Political Quarterly* (Blackwell Publishers, New York, 1983)

International Labour Office. *The TVA – Lessons for International Application* (ILO, Montreal, 1944)

Johannisson, B. and Nilsson, A. *Community Entrepreneurs: Networking for Local Development* in *Journal of Entrepreneurship and Regional Development* (Taylor and Francis, London, 1989)

Lasswell, H. *Power and Personality* (W.W. Norton, New York, 1948)

Lee, J. *Ireland, 1912–1985, Politics and Society* (Cambridge University Press, 1989)

Lichfield, N. *Report and Advisory Outline Plan for the Limerick Region* (Government Publications, Dublin, 1967)

McKee, D., Dean, R. and Leahy, W. *Regional Economics: Theory and Practice* (Free Press, New York, 1970)

Meindl, J. *The Romance of Leadership* in *Administrative Science Quarterly* (Cornell University, California, 1985)

Merton, R. *Social Theory and Social Structure* (Free Press, New York, 1957)

Micks, W. *History of the Congested Districts Board* (Eason and Son, Dublin, 1925)

Mulcahy, N. *SPS Case Study* (University of Limerick, Limerick, 1985)

Myrdal, G. *Economic Theory and Underdeveloped Regions* (Buckworth, London, 1957)

National Economic and Social Council. *A Review of Industrial Policy* (Government Publications, Dublin, 1982)

Neuse, S. 'TVA at Age Fifty – Reflections and Retrospect' in *Public Administration Review* (American Society for Public Administration, New York, 1983)

Nystrom, P. and Starbuck, W. *Handbook of Organisational Design, Volume 1* (Oxford University Press, New York, 1981)

O'Brien, D. 'The Social Networks of Leaders in More and Less Viable Rural Communities' in *Journal of Rural Sociology* (Boston, 1991)

OECD *Manpower Policy in Ireland* (Paris, 1974)

OECD *Innovation Policy in Ireland* (Paris, 1987)

OECD *Economic Outlook* (Paris, 1990)

O'Malley, E. *Free Trade Zones in Ireland and Four Asian Countries* (Trocaire Development Review, Dublin, 1986)

Perroux, F. *Note on the Concept of Growth Poles* (translated from *Economie Applique*, 1955, in McKee, op cit)

Pinchot, G. *Intrapreneuring* (Harper and Row, New York, 1985)

Podbielski, G. *Twenty Five Years of Special Action for the Development of Southern Italy* (Giuffre Editore, Rome, 1978)

Porter, M. *The Competitiveness of Nations* (Macmillan, London, 1990)

Posner, R. 'Theories of Economic Regulation' in *Bell Journal of Management and Economic Science* (Rand Corporation, New York, 1974)

Poulton, M. 'The Case for a Positive Theory of Planning' in *Environment and Planning* (Pion, London, 1991)

Rost, J. *Leadership for the Twenty-First Century* (Praeger, New York, 1991)

Ryan, L. *Shannon – Ireland's New Town* (University College Cork, Cork, 1968)

Santaniello, G. 'Extraordinary Intervention in the Mezzogiorno' in *Journal of Mezziorgiorno d'Europa* (Isveimer, Rome, 1983)

Sanyal, B. 'Ideas and Institutions: Why the Alternative Development Paradigm Withered Away' in *Regional Development Dialogue* (United Nations, New York, 1994)

Sashkin, M. 'True Vision in Leadership' in *Training and Development Journal* (Blackwell, London, 1986)

Sawhill, I. 'Strengthening the Three-Legged Stool of Policy Analysis, Organisation and Leadership' in *Journal of Policy Analysis and Management* (John Wiley, Washington DC, 1989)

Seers, D. 'The New Meaning of Development' in *International Development Review* (Sage, London, 1977)

Selznick, P. *Leadership in Administration* (Harper and Row, New York, 1957)

Selznick, P. *TVA and the Grass Roots* (Harper, New York, 1966)

Share, B. *Shannon Departures: A Study in Regional Initiatives* (Gill and Macmillan, Dublin, 1992)

Smith, P. and Peterson, M. *Leadership, Organisations and Culture* (Sage, London, 1988)

Sooklal, L. 'The Leader as a Broker of Dreams' in *Human Relations* (Plenum, London, 1991)

Stohr, W. and Taylor, R. *Development from Above or Below?* (Wiley, Chichester, 1981)

Stohr, W. 'Regional Innovation Complexes' in *Papers of the Regional Science Association* (Regional Science Association, London, 1986)

Thorelli, H. 'Networks: Between Markets and Hierarchies' in *Strategic Management Journal* (John Wiley, New York, 1986)

Tierney, J. 'Government Corporations and Managing the Public's Business' in *Political Science Quarterly* (Academy of Political Science, New York, 1984)

Tucker, R. *Personality and Political Leadership* in *Political Science* Quarterly (Academy of Political Science, New York, 1977)

Turpin, D. *Development Agencies and Regional Planning* (Paper to the European Congress of Development Agencies, Brussels, 1991)

Tushman, M. *The Management of Organisations* (Harper and Row, New York, 1989)

Valesco, R. *The Role of Regional Development Agencies in Promoting Economic Development in Objective 1 Regions* (Paper to the European Congress of Development Agencies, Brussels, 1991)

Westley, F. and Mintzberg, H. 'Visionary Leadership and Strategic Management' in *Strategic Management Journal* (John Wiley, New York, 1989)

Yin, R. *Case Study Research: Design and Methods* (Sage, California, 1989)

Index